PROJECT L.U.C.I.D.

PROJECT L.U.C.I.D.

The Beast 666 Universal Human Control System

TEXE MARRS

LTP Living Truth Publishers
1708 Patterson Road • Austin, Texas 78733

ACKNOWLEDGEMENTS

How truly grateful I am for the many, wonderful people who have done so much to help me research, format, and produce this book. First in my heart, of course, is my wife, Wanda. Without her love and support, *Project L.U.C.I.D.* would never have seen the light of day. My incomparable staff deserves credit: Sandra Schappert, Kimberly Reiley, Joe Saldaña, Michelle Delgado, Gerry Schappert, and Aron Brackeen.

A special thanks goes to Terry Cook, whose keen insight over the years on this subject has been truly inspirational. Also, to the many others who kindly send me valuable research materials and information, I say: God bless you!

Project L.U.C.I.D.—The Beast 666 Universal Human Control System

Scripture quotations are from the King James Version of The Holy Bible.

L.U.C.I.D.® is a registered trademark of the Advanced Technologies Group, Inc., New Rochelle, New York. Wherever the name or title, L.U.C.I.D., is found in this book or on its cover, the trademark provisions of law apply.

Cover design: Texe Marrs, Wanda Marrs and Sandra Schappert

Cover graphic by Brian Godawa

Printed in the United States of America

Library of Congress Catalog Card Number 96-77122

Categories: 1. Current Events and Issues   2. Computers
3. Technology and Science   4. Politics
5. Prophecy

ISBN 1-884302-02-5

"A frightening behemoth is rising up from the depths of America's hidden *SS* establishment. Like a vast and monstrous silicon octopus, ***Project L.U.C.I.D.*** is stretching forth its ominous and threatening, high tech tentacles. Multitudes of unsuspecting, helpless victims will very soon be encircled and crushed by Big Brother's new, Gestapo police state. Who among us can possibly escape from the electronic cages now being prepared for all mankind?"

—Texe Marrs

OTHER BOOKS BY TEXE MARRS

Circle of Intrigue: The Hidden Inner Circle of the Global Illuminati Conspiracy

Big Sister Is Watching You: Hillary Clinton and the White House Feminists Who Now Control America— And Tell the President What to Do

Dark Majesty: The Secret Brotherhood and the Magic of A Thousand Points of Light

Millennium: Peace, Promises, and the Day They Take Our Money Away

America Shattered

New Age Cults and Religions

Ravaged by the New Age

Mystery Mark of the New Age

Dark Secrets of the New Age

Mega Forces

FOR TEXE MARRS' FREE NEWSLETTER

For a free subscription to *Flashpoint*, Texe Marrs' international newsletter, please phone 1-800-234-9673 or write to:

Living Truth Publishers
1708 Patterson Road
Austin, Texas 78733

Please e-mail your request to: livingtr@io.com, or visit us at our internet website: http://www.texemarrs.com

CONTENTS

We Knew It Was Coming

The *Beast 666 Universal Human Control System* has been designed and is being implemented in America and throughout the world. We knew it was coming. Now it's here, and soon, there will be no place left to hide. By the year 2000, Big Brother's evil, octopus-like tentacles will squeeze every ounce of lifeblood out of the people. A nightmarish, totalitarian police state is at hand.

That is the thoroughly documented message—and momentous warning—sounded in this book. Do not for an instant think that *you and your loved ones* can escape the monstrous behemoth which lies in our path. Once *Project L.U.C.I.D.* is fully operational, every man, woman, and child will fall under the power of its hideous, cyber-electronic grasp.

The Magnitude and Dimensions of Project L.U.C.I.D.

Consider the unbelievable magnitude and dimensions of *Project L.U.C.I.D.* First, it mandates that every adult and child—even newborn babies—be issued a *universal biometrics I.D. card*. A "Smart Card" with an advanced computer microchip, this powerful, reprogrammable I.D. card will store millions of bytes of information about the recipient—his or her photo, fingerprint, footprint, iris (eye) scan, DNA genotype, human leukocyte antigen data, financial status, and personal history. Oh yes, the I.D. card will also be coded with *numbers*. One will identify the individual card holder. Another, I believe, will eventually constitute the number 666. The number 666 will signify the hellish master responsible for the devilish invention of this Universal Biometrics Card and its interlocked, computer network.

L.U.C.I.D. establishes a massive, Big Brother, computer database of unparalleled, invasive power. Millions of bureaucrats employed by a hidden, SS Gestapo establishment will constantly feed this electronic Beast with more and more data. They will hungrily and rapaciously tap into its billions of cyberspace-filed dossiers, searching for information by which they can extend the Beast's dominion and influence into every nook and cranny of our lives.

L.U.C.I.D.'s cyberspace dossiers will be made instantly available to thousands of probing, faceless, police state agents and bureaucrats around the globe. America's CIA, IRS, and FBI, the Russian KGB, Europe's Interpol and Europol, Israel's Mossad, Britain's military intelligence—these are just a few of the planetary-wide law enforcement, military, and intelligence agencies having access to your dossier and to mine.

A Central Gestapo Repository

Moreover, all biographical data and personal information about you will be linked, networked, and processed by a *Central Gestapo* repository. Into the abyss of its databanks will flow never-ending streams of information—countless trillions of bits of data—instantly, steadily, and stealthily accumulating and accumulating.

The information will come in from laser scanners at supermarkets, department stores, and direct-mail houses which record every single item you purchase. Data about your daily habits and movements will flow into the Beast system from spy satellites, constantly circling overhead, watching us all like the squinting eyes of a giant, soaring eagle, ready to pounce and consume its hapless victims. Hidden, miniature video cameras will be recording our activities, indoors and outdoors, day and night, obscenely invading our privacy and instantaneously transmitting their mountainous files of recorded, visual data to the Central Gestapo by the miraculous use of fiber optics lines.

Interactive TV sets will be watching us just as we watch them—and they'll report back to the Beast Computer at headquarters.

Our telephone conversations will be automatically wiretapped and transcripted by the National Security Agency, then digitally sent on their way via the Information Superhighway, each being sequentially stored and accessible on the *L.U.C.I.D.* net. Everything, in fact, will be duly recorded, stored, and accessed at will by the technocratic agents who administer this monstrous system, *L.U.C.I.D.*

While the high tech cops and their remote sensors, operating under *L.U.C.I.D.*, watch and monitor our personal lives, our material goods will also be receiving the careful and meticulous scrutiny of the Gestapo agents who operate and wield the magic tools of cyberspace. A mark or certification of approval is to be given every facility where manufactured products come off an assembly line. Every gadget, every part, every device, every machine, every item of clothing, every piece of jewelry, every tool—in fact, all goods—will come under the authority of the *ISO 9000* program. A government inspector must put his mark of certification on the facility making a product *or it cannot be bought and sold.*

"But," the skeptic may say, "the system described here, codenamed *Project L.U.C.I.D.*, is so draconian, so horrendously unconstitutional, that the people of America would never go for it. They would never allow such a Beast Computer system to be built and used."

What naivete! As I will demonstrate in this book, the Beast system is not only being constructed, its employment against Americans and against citizens of every nation on earth is inevitable. *Project L.U.C.I.D.* will prove to be Lucifer's end-times identification, surveillance, and control system.

God's Prophetic Blueprint

To enable readers to grasp the inevitability of this malignant system of totalitarian control, we must turn our attention to God's prophetic blueprint for the last days. The United Nations, the United States of America, and the political leader of every country on this planet have no choice but to rigorously and exactly fulfill the prophetic scenario for the last days, as prescribed with astonishing clarity in God's biblical blueprint—miraculously given to His prophets thousands of years in advance!

Bible prophecy, with its stupendous, heart-gripping vision of a perilous future, reveals that the end time will be a tumultuous period of deception and betrayal. A strong delusion (II Thessalonians 2:11) will overtake the minds of men so that they will willingly worship the Dragon (Satan) and the Beast, also known as the Antichrist (Revelation 13). They will also pay homage to his global New World Order. People everywhere will wondrously proclaim, "Who is like unto the Beast? who is able to make war with him" (Revelation 13:4)?

This they will do even though the Beast is given "a mouth speaking great things and blasphemies." This bold, but evil, man will even dare to open his mouth in blasphemy against God, "to blaspheme his name, and his tabernacle, and them that dwell in heaven" (Revelation 13:5-6).

Moreover, warns the Bible, "it was given unto him to make war with the saints, and to overcome them: and power was given him over all kindreds, and tongues, and nations" (Revelation 13:7). This, then, is a prophecy which reveals to us the incredible scope and dominion of the

Beast. His authority is to extend throughout the entire earth. He is to rule and reign over every race and over every nation.

Extraordinary Methods: A Mark and a Number

Never in human history has there been such a fantastic plot to handcuff and wrap modern men and women inside electronic, cyber-locked cages. Bible prophecy envisions a grotesque and amazing system of human control and enslavement. Is *Project L.U.C.I.D.* the chilling *Beast 666 Universal Human Control System* which, according to the Bible, is destined to "devour" the whole world and break it into pieces (Daniel 7:7)? Is *Project L.U.C.I.D.*, indeed, the fulfillment of the breathtaking prophecies of the Antichrist, 666, recorded in the book of *Revelation?*:

> Here is wisdom. Let him that hath understanding count the number of the beast: for it is the number of a man; and his number is Six hundred threescore and six. (Revelation 13:18)

In studying prophecy, we discover that, to cement and strengthen his authority over the lives and fortunes of men and women, the Beast will, in that savage time of brutality and awesome, Big Brother dictatorship, organize the financial systems and *commerce* of the whole world (Revelation 18). Moreover, by minutely and totally *controlling all purchases,* the watchful, all seeing eye of the Beast ceaselessly glances and turns to and fro, capturing every person in its terrible sight: *"...that no man might buy or sell, save he that had the mark, or the name of the beast, or the number of his name"* (Revelation 13:17).

Remember, this does not come from some "wild-eyed conspiracy theorist," as the controlled media are prone to describe it. This shocking, eye-opening prophecy comes straight from the mind of God. *He says it will happen, and it will.*

The Military Wizards of Invention

For over 20 years in the U.S. Air Force, I observed fantastic, technological advances come to reality—laser-guided "smart" munitions; missile warning radars; spy satellites; neutron bombs; remotely piloted vehicles (drone aircraft); Mirv'd ICBM platforms; and incredible, electronic, "killer" gadgetry that defies the imagination.

I recall driving each day past the huge and monstrously solemn building at Lackland Air Force Base where young warriors train in the latest cryptographic equipment and techniques. My mind goes back to the highly classified building in Italy—lacking windows, surrounded by barbed wire, patrolled by security police, and fortified by concrete—in which I toiled for many months. Inside, powerful, room-sized computers hummed and buzzed as electronic communications machines—seeming to come straight out of some futuristic, *Buck Rogers* movie—monitored climactic events occurring across the globe.

Stationed in Germany, I was the commander of hundreds of technicians and specialists who traveled throughout Europe and the Middle East, establishing classified communications links and transmitting cryptologically encoded messages back and forth on secure lines.

At the University of Texas at Austin for five years, I taught officer cadets American defense policy, the organization of the Air Force, and the history of aviation and aerospace. I also imparted to them knowledge of military strategy and tactics and introduced them to a wide range of new, *Star Wars*-era aircraft and armaments. We even game-played, "How to Fight and Win World War III."

Futurism and Technology

Later, following my retirement as a U.S. Air Force officer, I put my technological knowledge to effective use, founding my own, high tech consulting firm, Tech Trends. As president of Tech Trends, I was privileged to meet and share information with some of America's best, technological minds. I was also kept busy researching and writing books on futuristic high technology for major New York publishers such as Stein & Day, Simon Schuster, Prentice-Hall, McGraw-Hill/Tab Books, Dow Jones-Irwin, Barron's, and Facts on File. Among those books:

Robotica: The Whole Universe Catalog of Robots
The Personal Robot Book
Careers in Computers
High Technology Job Finder
High Technology Careers
Careers With Robots

My investigations took me to research laboratories and exotic corporate locales, where I became privy to mind-boggling information about horrendously destructive, high technology systems on the drawing boards. In the last few years, I have steadily seen those same, dark systems introduced in the public marketplace, often presented as something positive, good, and beneficial for the progress and prosperity of mankind.

This is why *L.U.C.I.D.*, the advanced computer technology, global control system outlined in this book, comes as no surprise to me. The Holy Bible prophesied of its emergence in the last days. My experiences in the Air Force and in the high tech consulting and writing field forewarned me.

But unlike the government bureaucrats and the corporate promoters—who stand to wield awesome power and acquire tremendous wealth from the *L.U.C.I.D.* system—I do not share the same, rosy view of this system's many, so-called benefits. I am, instead, horrified that the American people are about to enter a sinister period of blood, terror, and slavery unparalleled in human history. Worse, the vast majority are *totally unprepared* for what is to come.

To Make the People Happy

In his book, *The Permanent Revolution: The French Revolution and Its Legacy*, Professor George Steiner paints a grim picture of a brief episode in history in which *all things changed abruptly—almost overnight.* The upheaval in France was so brutal, and so wrenching, that the entire social, political, economic, and religious order was turned on its head. Blood flowed from the guillotine; men feasted on savage acts of barbarism and cruelty while the screams and cries of the tortured, dying victims were either muted or laughed at.[1]

And all this was done to make the people happy and to insure their prosperous and contented future! As one, revolutionary, Illuminati/Jacobin leader, Frenchman Rabaud de Saint Etienne exclaimed:

> To make the people happy, their ideas must be reconstructed, laws must be changed, morals must be changed, men must be changed, things must be changed, yes everything must be destroyed, since everything must be remade.[2]

Today, in the final years of the turbulent and eventful 20th century, we once again are hearing insistent demands for a "New Civilization," a "New Age," a "Paradigm Shift," a "New Way of Thinking." We are told that, yes, all things must change—and men must change. The world must be "reinvented;" a newfound "Politics of Meaning" is in order, a "New Covenant."

These changes are necessary, we are reminded each day by our mind control jailers in the media, to solve the immigration crisis, to institute gun control, to counter domestic terrorism, to fight pornography, to find deadbeat dads who don't pay child support, to "Save Mother Earth," to protect endangered species, to war against drug kingpins, to stop crime in the streets, to watch and monitor the militias, to prevent ethnic cleansing and tribal rivalries, to put an end to hate crimes and bigotry, to extend universal healthcare benefits, to guarantee welfare reform, to improve public education...The list of crises and problems to be fixed seems to be never-ending.

The Grand Solution

And so, to make the people happy, the leaders of our Big Brother government, who love us all so very dearly, have come up with a solution which can solve many, if not most, of our problems. I call it *Project L.U.C.I.D.* This involves an array of black science tools and Big Brother electronic devices. Implement *this* system, they promise, and a bright, secure future can be ours.

A key component of this larger control system is *L.U.C.I.D.* net, a universal system of linked databases. Its sponsors claim it will be a godsend to the global law enforcement community, especially in fighting international and domestic terrorism. Strangely, however, *L.U.C.I.D.* net requires computer registration, constant electronic surveillance, and a microchip-integrated Universal Biometrics I.D. Card for every *child* born on planet earth! Why do *babies* need to be tracked and monitored? Is there any known case in the annals of criminal history in which a *baby* in a cradle committed some heinous act of global terrorism?

The designers of *L.U.C.I.D.* net claim their system is only proposed, that it is not in operation at this time. Nonsense! The powers who rule over us are *already* implementing many aspects of this draconian, com-puterized control system. They are doing so without our permission and, for the most part, without our knowledge!

If you complain, they will tell you, of course, that they are doing this for your own good, that their control sensors will guarantee you security and safety. Once *L.U.C.I.D.* is fully in operation, they add, it will help solve all those terrible crises the press keeps telling you about. The computer, they trumpet, is an instrument only of good. It is necessary to make you *happy!*

Sacrifices Required to Baal

However, in their book, *Computer Consciousness*, authors H. Dominic Corvey and Neil McAlister sound words of caution: "If we fail to fear the computer's ability to become a latter-day Baal who demands our sacrifices on the altar of technology," they warn, "then we may, unresistingly, become first its worshippers, and finally its sacrifices."[3]

Please, I beg you, read *Project L.U.C.I.D.* carefully and prayerfully. Sincerely ask yourself, "Is this not the setting up of the *Beast 666 Universal Human Control System* prophesied in the book of *Revelation?* Do we not have something to fear from "the computer's ability to become a latter-day Baal?" Might we, unless we resist, "become first its worshippers, and finally its sacrifices?"

Know the Truth—and Prepare!

It is, today, most unpopular to present—as I have here—a message of "gloom and doom." Men everywhere seem to be caught up in denial. They fear the awful truth; therefore, they avoid it and cast it from their minds and consciousness. Would it not be better, however, to know the truth, to discover the worst, and provide for it?

Patrick Henry, America's great orator and patriot of the Revolutionary War against the tyrannical regime of Britain's King George III, once made a stirring declaration of where he stood on such matters. My prayer is that, as you read and study the pages that follow, you will take to heart his inspiring and uplifting words. Patrick Henry, history records, was a man who rejected the threats and seductions of Baal. He loved Jesus Christ and was willing to follow the Truth, even to the death. In one of his most famous and beloved speeches, Patrick Henry said this:

> It is natural to man to indulge in the illusions of hope. We are apt to shut our eyes against a painful truth, and listen to the song of that siren, till she transforms us into

beasts. Is this the part of wise men, engaged in a great and arduous struggle for liberty? Are we disposed to be of the number of those who, having eyes, see not, and having ears, hear not, the things which so nearly concern their temporal salvation? For my part, whatever anguish of spirit it may cost, I am willing to know the whole truth; to know the worst and to provide for it.[4]

—Texe Marrs
Austin, Texas

ONE

Project L.U.C.I.D.—
The Beast 666 Universal
Human Control System

Astonishing and undeniable evidence exists of an incredible, new "Beast 666 Universal Human Control System." Officially called *L.U.C.I.D.*, it is a grotesque system of universal slavery which—even as you read this—is being implemented by federal and international intelligence police agencies. The Beast 666 system mandates that every man, woman, and child on planet earth be issued a high tech, "Smart" I.D. card, called a *Universal Biometrics Card*. The chilling system is slated to be fully in operation by the year 2000, to celebrate the dawn of the New Age Millennium.

This computerized I.D. card—to be followed eventually by an implanted biochip—is an electronic straitjacket that allows the New World Order's Gestapo to track and link every man, woman, and child on planet earth. Our activities are going to be monitored 24 hours a day, seven days a week, by federal Gestapo agencies—the FBI, IRS, BATF, CIA, DIA, DEA, NSA, NRO, FINCEN, the U.S. Treasury Service, the Department of Justice, and countless other alphabet spook and police agencies. Their numbers multiply almost weekly!

International police and intelligence agencies will also be linked with the Beast 666 system, to include America's Big Brother-enforcing CIA, the vicious Russian KGB, the devious and wicked British Intelligence Service, and Israel's terroristic and bloody Mossad spy organization.

No Privacy with the Orwellian "Beast I.D." System

The computerized *Universal Biometrics Card* guarantees the control and surveillance of every living human being. The card will contain templates, or samples, of the "individual's DNA genotype" and his or her "human leukocyte antigen." The artificial intelligence software and special sensors loaded into the card will also implement a number of other identification methods, including the capture of such human features as profile and facial photos, fingerprints, footprints, and iris scans of the eye.

A computerized, pen-like, fiber-optic and laser camera will be used at I.D. card issuing centers to be set up around the world. All citizens will be ordered to report to these centers and "volunteer" their bodies to the camera devices so that the I.D. card can instantly be manufactured and issued. Babies born in the future will immediately be entered into the system at hospitals and other birthing centers.

Massive, Global Computer System Established

Sophisticated, international, computerized, telecommunications and intelligence gathering centers have already been established in preparation for the issuance of the new, human control cards. The world's most advanced super computers are being utilized. All spy information acquired on humans, plus the future data from their *Universal Biometrics Card*, is to be fed into the gigantic network, which is called the *Universal Computerized Identification Clearinghouse Resource Center*. This center is the very heart of the evil *L.U.C.I.D.*, or Beast 666 Universal Human Control System. *L.U.C.I.D.*, reports one reliable source, is an interactive and instantaneous *tracking system* of all living

L.U.C.I.D.© &
The Counter-Terrorism Act Of 1995

Presented by:

Jean Paul Creusat, M.D., L.U.C.I.D.© System Designer;Medical Officer Investigator on Narcotics Control and INEOA Representative to the United Nations NGO- ECOSOC.
Anthony S. Halaris, M.S., Iona College Computer Science Professor, Information Systems Specialist and President of Advanced Technologies Group Inc, New Rochelle, New York, U.S.A.

KEY WORDS

National Crime Information Center (NCIC) 2000; Integrated Automated Fingerprint Identification System (IAFIS); National Instant Criminal Background (NICB); Interstate Identification Index (III) or Triple I;

ABSTRACT

L.U.C.I.D.© is a concept study for a future Universal Information Identification System via L.U.C.I.D.© Net. This article intends to advocate the research and development of this system to help prevent, deter and frustrate terrorism and international organized crime. L.U.C.I.D.© System will be an all-source fusion information center that will interface multilingual messages into a common communications network.

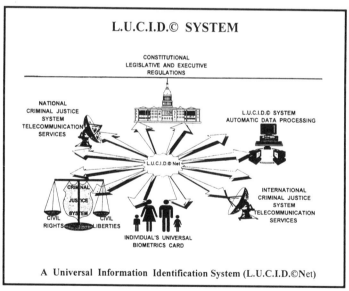

L.U.C.I.D.© SYSTEM

A Universal Information Identification System (L.U.C.I.D.©Net)

Information about the L.U.C.I.D. system was published in the Narc Officer magazine. Included was this shocking chart depicting how a typical family—husband, wife and two kids—is to be minutely controlled by I.D. cards linked with the global net.

beings on earth. It is designed so that no one can escape its clutches. *No one!*

Gestapo Agencies to Arrest Anti-Government Suspects

While its designers would deny it, I believe that federal and international Gestapo agencies will use the instantaneous information maintained on file at the Beast 666 universal computer center to trace, investigate, monitor, spy on, arrest, and incarcerate "resisters." From the highly confidential, insider information I have privately received, it is obvious that resisters are categorized as: "Any and all persons who protest or oppose the Illuminati's fascist agenda for the New World Order."

Recently introduced, so-called "anti-terrorist" legislation, plus the Omnibus Anti-Crime Bill of 1994, are the catalysts which make possible the immediate arrest and imprisonment of any and all persons *suspected* of being a "terrorist." These persons shall be deemed as "risks to internal security."

Significantly, the arrest of a targeted Christian, patriot, or other citizen will take place *whether or not* that person has actually committed a criminal act. "Thought crimes" alone provide justification for the arrest of dissidents. Arrests of targeted citizens are to be euphemistically called "preventive detention."

Homes and Other Private Property Will Be Seized

The person's home, auto, bank account, and other property shall be seized. This will be accomplished under existing *forfeiture laws*, originally designed to stop drug dealers and kingpins, but now being used across America by Gestapo police to harass and bankrupt private citizens opposed to Big Brother government's criminal activities. These forfeiture laws are conveniently used by federal agencies and local law enforcement authorities throughout the 50 states to grab the property of people not guilty of any crime. No court order, no warrant, is needed.

Recently, treasonous federal courts have ripped to shreds over 200 years of American constitutional law, ruling that, "A person's property has no constitutional rights."

Processing Centers...or Concentration Camps?

Individuals who have been arrested and their property seized and sold at auction, will then be transported with other dissidents by truck, bus, and air to a FEMA-managed, regional *Federal Prison Transfer Center* for proper "categorization" and "disposition." Entire families are to be disposed of in this manner. Neighbors and the local communities will be given the excuse that the surviving spouses and children of those arrested are being "assisted" by the government.

Final disposition, when deemed appropriate, will be made at a regional *Processing and Detention Center*. The Nazis called such centers *concentration camps*. In the Soviet Union, they were known as *gulags*. At these "Centers," methods and techniques of interrogation, torture, and final disposition honed and developed by the CIA and Special Forces Green Berets through their *Operation Phoenix* program are to be used on victimized citizens. During the Vietnam conflict, the federal government's Top Secret, *Operation Phoenix* program was responsible for the arrest, incarceration, torture, and murder of over 50,000 innocent civilians. The CIA and U.S. Army Special Forces acclaimed it a success and a model and prototype for future "human pacification" programs.

For Your Own Protection and Safety

Preliminary information on *Project L.U.C.I.D.* is even now being disseminated to federal law enforcement agencies.

It can be expected that managers of these agencies will be briefed on how to use coverup propaganda to cleverly respond to public and local press inquiries, so that the awful truth will not become known until it is too late. For example, government PR experts will reassure the frightened and startled masses that, "all constitutional protections remain in place."

Worried citizens are also to be advised that the new system is designed to "protect them" from savage acts by international and domestic terrorists, such as occurred in the Oklahoma City and New York's World Trade Center bombings. The public is to be conned into believing that *"L.U.C.I.D.* is for your own good, and anyone who says differently is either a conspiracy nut or a dangerous, anti-government protester."

God Warned This Day Would Come!

The Bible predicted that an end-times Beast 666 Universal Human Control System would be used to control and enslave humanity: "That no man might buy or sell, save he that had the mark, or the name of the beast, or the number of his name" (Revelation 13:17). Now it's here!

I believe that *Project L.U.C.I.D.* will be implemented at the direction of the *Inner Circle* of the Illuminati. The system has been developed and is being installed by Fascist international corporations and banks, working jointly with United Nations consultants, U.S. intelligence bureaucrats and overseers, and law enforcement personnel. *Project L.U.C.I.D.* is Satan's diabolical, end-times system of total and absolute human control. It will put mankind under direct subjection to the Antichrist and his jackbooted, Gestapo-thug storm troopers. Every government on earth will cooperate with the New World Order system and act to oppress its citizens. All governments and corporations everywhere will have access to the *L.U.C.I.D.* net. *There will be nowhere to hide!*

Purging and Cleansing

The purging and cleansing of planet earth is at hand. The Beast intends to be rid of such dynamic "enemies of the state" as Christian separatists, patriots, and nationalists. Every nation on earth will join in this campaign to eradicate the "human vermin and diseased human rats" who, it is said, now infect the wounded, sacred body of Mother Earth. *Project L.U.C.I.D.* is vividly bringing to pass Daniel 7:25 which reveals that the Beast:

> ...shall speak great words against the Most High, and shall wear out the saints of the most High, and think to change times and laws: and they shall be given into his hand until a time and times and the dividing of time.

This cardinal development in human control signals the rapid, breathtaking emergence of the end-times Beast. His universal system is described by the Bible as "dreadful and terrible." The awesome power of the global Beast system is such that it "devoured and brake in pieces, and stamped the residue" of the saints with its feet (Daniel 7:7).

"The Wise Shall Understand"

Why do I publish these frightening facts about *Project L.U.C.I.D.*—facts which, admittedly, are both alarming and stupefying—though absolutely true? My friends, it is our duty to warn those who dwell in unbelief that the time is upon us. Some will wisely understand and prepare by taking shelter in Jesus Christ. He alone provides help and protection. Others will scoff and denounce us as fanatics. Then, they will prance off to continue their wicked lifestyle and worldly ways. But, this, too was prophesied in God's Word. Only the chosen, the *wise*—those who know and believe in our Lord Jesus Christ—will understand, and this is as it should be. For we read that, in the final, momentous days:

> Many shall be purified, and made white, and tried; but the wicked shall do wickedly: and none of the wicked shall understand; but the wise shall understand. (Daniel 12:10)

There is much, much more about *Project L.U.C.I.D.* that you need to know. I believe that the insider information we have obtained is tremendously important, unbelievably vital, and earthshaking. So, let us begin to unravel the mind-boggling secrets our elitist controllers do not want you to know!

Who is Responsible for Project L.U.C.I.D.?

The project to control the people of the world through universal computer identification and tracking systems first began in the twisted minds of high-level, New World Order planners of America's super-secretive *National Security Agency (NSA)*. The NSA is an agency employing thousands of government bureaucrats, intelligence officials, military personnel, and technological specialists in a global-wide operation. Its headquarters, closely guarded by U.S. Army security personnel at Fort Meade, Maryland, is housed in the second largest building in the United States, surpassed only by the Pentagon in Washington, D.C. This huge, behemoth of a facility, appropriately enough, has been called the "Puzzle Palace."

The mission of the NSA, broad and all-encompassing, involves war planning, security investigation, classified materials control, and management of America's far-flung spy and intelligence network. The CIA, the State Department, even the White House and its occupants, take orders from the chiefs at the NSA.

In the international arena, the NSA is master of all it surveys. Every major foreign intelligence agency and law enforcement bureau is charged with keeping the computer czars of the NSA informed at all times of their activities. This supervision and control also extends to the chiefs of internal security and the heads of justice departments and bureaus in every nation in Europe, North, South and Central America, and Asia. The infamous activities and international crimes of France's intelligence service, Russia's KGB secret police, Israel's spy agency, the Mossad, Britain's MI-6, and Canada's Secret Intelligence Service (CSIS) can all be laid at the feet of America's notoriously evil National Security Agency.

The whirring of the computers and the eerie sounds emanating from the ultra-classified, cryptographic machines inside the NSA's Puzzle Palace never cease. Twenty-four hours a day, the NSA hums along, its giant computer network correlating, deciphering, and analyzing data and reports from international banks, from the 32 directorates of the United Nations, and from the bowels of the Secret Societies, the Vatican curia, and the various agencies of over 170 nations around the globe.

The Fount of Global Evil

This hulking monstrosity is currently the fount of global evil for the New World Order, which some now euphemistically call the "New Civilization." It is responsible for genocidal massacres of hundreds of thousands of people in Rwanda, Burundi, and Angola in Africa, for the brutal ethnic cleansing and killing camps in Bosnia, and for the bloody, experimental concentration camp operation run by NSA stooge Jim Jones of the Peoples Temple, in Guyana, South America.

Based on a growing mountain of evidence, I am also convinced that the National Security Agency, through its subsidiary, servant organizations in America, the CIA, FBI, DOJ, BATF, IRS, etc., is guilty of horrific, murderous and barbaric acts of terrorism everywhere on planet earth. With their so-called "black budgets," the NSA and its inferior organizations sponsor, create, fund, and manage terror units and groups of all ideological stripes and shades, from left-wing Communist to right-wing Fascist, from Arab-

A rare photo of the National Security Agency (NSA) complex at Fort Meade, Maryland.

Popular Mechanics carried this feature article on America's spy satellite. With the end of the Cold War, these sophisticated, spy satellites are now used to spy on individual citizens.

Islamic to Jewish, and from white supremacist to black separatist.

But the chief and most strategic mission of the labyrinth known as the National Security Agency is the development and oversight of the construction of the Beast 666 Universal Human Control System.

Through its supervision of the *Defense Advanced Research Projects Agency (DARPA)*, with its own multibillion budget, the NSA has been able to create and install a fabulous, global system of computers, satellites, telecommunications devices, and surveillance gadgetry.

Since the 1970s, DARPA has been bursting at the seams with the billions of dollars thrown its way by our profligate, wastrel Congress. Ostensibly, this money went into the research and development of new and advanced, highly sophisticated military weaponry. And, in fact, DARPA has spent untold truckloads of cash developing laser death rays, weather weapons, electromagnetic field systems, reconnaissance satellites, etc. DARPA has also been the sugar daddy for the fabled *Star Wars* missile defense systems development.

However, unbeknown even to our ignorant and deceived U.S. Senators and Representatives, along with its defense projects, the men who plot behind the massive, locked doors of the NSA's Puzzle Palace have also spent as much as $250 billion dollars, spread over the past quarter of a century, to create systems of human control. Moreover, these systems are so diabolically masterful that only Satan himself could originally have conceived them.

Lucifer in Charge

There can be no doubt about it. The *real* Chief Executive Officer of the NSA is not a human being. The CEO *must*

For verification and documentation of the National Security Agency's dangerous, unconstitutional activities and role, please see the appendices at the back of this book.

be Lucifer himself. And though its human inventors insist otherwise, I believe that the acronym, *L.U.C.I.D.*, stands for *Lucifer's Universal Criminal Identification* System. (A short version is *Lucifer's* I.D. System!)

Note and beware the key word, "Criminal," which the letter "C" in *L.U.C.I.D.* denotes. In Lucifer's twisted philosophical paradigm and mind-set, it is the biblical Christian, above all others, who is the "criminal." Along with patriots and other resisters to the New World Order, the biblical Christian is to be culled out, persecuted, and neutralized. Ultimately, this identification, tracking, and monitoring of innocent, yet despised, Christian victims will result in the incarceration and death of untold masses.

If, however, you do not fit into the category of a biblical Christian or a patriotic resister to the New World Order, do not think you will escape the all seeing eye of Big Brother's *Project L.U.C.I.D.*

Dr. Antony Sutton, an expert on advanced and futuristic technology systems, says that *L.U.C.I.D.* may hone in on certain individuals whom the government feels are undesirables, but *everyone* will come under its authority and be subject to its high tech sensors.

Sutton, a highly astute researcher who authored *The Secret Establishment* and other books unmasking secret societies and exposing the aims of the globalists, is one of the tiny handful of men who have, so far, exposed the manifest dangers of *L.U.C.I.D.* He writes:

Big Brother planners have now excelled themselves with a totalitarian scheme to hook all of us up to a central computer tracking system, with the assumption that we are all criminals and need to be catalogued and tracked...

L.U.C.I.D. proposes that the Universal Biometrics Card *now under development by the Department of Defense* be used as "a secure, uniform, interactive, and instantaneous tracking system."

Tracking of whom you will ask? Not criminals, but according to its designers' own words, "noncriminal justice background checks" and "alias criminals." That means potentially everybody. We applaud their ingenious use of the English language. What's an "alias criminal?"[1]

The Meaning of L.U.C.I.D.

Why the acronym *L.U.C.I.D.?* What words do the cryptic letters respresnt? Dr. Sutton has taken note of this curious acronym, *L.U.C.I.D.* What does it mean? He observes that, "The word LUCID is notably close to LUCIS, or LUCIFER."

"We trust," Sutton writes, that "this was not a Freudian slip on the part of the (designer) authors."

Terry Cook, another researcher aware of the plan for *L.U.C.I.D.,* inquires: "So what does *L.U.C.I.D.* mean? What do the initials stand for? Nobody knows!" But Terry Cook has his suspicions, and he has also taken note of the "LUCID/LUCIS/LUCIFER connection."[2]

"According to *Webster's New Collegiate Dictionary,*" Cook writes, the word *lucid* means "suffused with light; luminous; translucent..." This, he suggests, gives us a definite clue that Lucifer may be lurking behind the scenes.[3]

The Bible cautions that Satan, or Lucifer, does, indeed, often come cloaked innocuously and deceptively as an emissary of goodness and righteousness. He and his ministers do not appear as conspiratorial, scheming devils and as wicked men, but as *"angels of light"* (II Corinthians 11:14). Thus it is that in every occult system, the priest and theologians emphasize the desire to seek after *"more light."*

Both Sutton and Cook mention also the premier occultic organization known as *Lucis Trust,* incorporated in 1922 as *Lucifer Publishing* and located on United Nations Plaza in New York City. In my books, *Dark Secrets of the New Age, Mystery Mark of the New Age, New Age Cults and Religions,* and others, I examine the Lucis Trust and its subsidiary organizations. I show that it is closely affiliated with the United Nations leadership and that the Lucis Trust's membership includes powerful men such as Robert McNamara, former Secretary of Defense and former head of the World Bank. The Lucis Trust is formally accredited as a "nongovernmental organization (NGO) of the United Nations." I also prove that its name, *Lucis*, is derived from combining the names of Lucifer (the sun deity) and Isis (the great goddess of Egypt). Lucis Trust tells inquirers that the name stems from the Latin word for "light" or "light-bearing."

Terry Cook points out that in the symbol of the Lucis Trust logo are concealed the letters L, U, and X, or LUX, which, in Latin, means "light."

The overriding goal of the Lucis Trust is a New World Order made up of a "Thousand Points of Light." (Some claim that the founder of Lucis Trust, theosophist Alice Bailey, coined the term, "New World Order.")This New World Order will be presided over by a New Age Christ, or Messiah, soon to come, who will govern a united humanity with principles based on occult, magic, and science.

I cannot say for sure if the designers of the *L.U.C.I.D.* network, Dr. Anthony Halaris and Dr. Jean-Paul Creusat, are members of the Lucis Trust, or of one of its several subsidiary organizations. But we should perhaps note that while the corporation, Advanced Technologies Group, Inc., which claims authorship of *L.U.C.I.D.*, is variously listed by internet directories as being headquartered in either West Des Moines, Iowa or Lombard, Illinois, Dr. Halaris, who serves as president of the firm, lists his address as New Rochelle, New York. This is the same state where the Lucis Trust is headquartered. Halaris is also listed as a computer science professor at Iona College in New York state.

Meanwhile, Dr. Creusat is a medical doctor who officially holds the positions of "L.U.C.I.D. System Designer." He also is on the staff of Interpol as a "Medical Officer Investigator on Narcotics Control," and is an "International Narcotics Enforcement Officers Association

(INEOA) Representative to the United Nations NGO-ECOSOC." [4] *ECOSOC* stands for *Economic and Social Council of the United Nations.* In short, Dr. Creusat is an official representative of a foreign police agency working with a nongovernmental organization (NGO) of the United Nations. As I mentioned, the Lucis Trust is *also* accredited as a NGO of the United Nations.

Unraveling a Mystery

It is apparent to me that, as researcher Antony Sutton and Terry Cook discovered, designers Creusat and Halaris are very reluctant to reveal the true meaning of the acronym, *L.U.C.I.D.* It took all of my investigative skills to elicit a formal response from these men to my simple request for information. First, my office personally contacted Dr. Anthony Halaris at Iona College. "What does *'L.U.C.I.D.'* stand for?," we inquired. The secretive Halaris refused to say, but, instead referred us to Dr. Jean-Paul Creusat, his associate.

We were able to locate Dr. Creusat at a company called Birkmayer Software Development in New York City. (Is Birkmayer yet another CIA proprietary organization?) When Creusat refused to talk to us, we interviewed a "Mr. Bernardo Lam," a technical specialist at the firm.

Even though he admitted working closely with Dr. Creusat in the development of the *L.U.C.I.D.* software project, Lam insisted he did not know what the acronym stood for. He did confirm to us that Dr. Creusat works for *Interpol,* the international police agency, with headquarters in Paris, France. Mr. Lam also said, regarding *L.U.C.I.D.,* that Dr. Creusat was the chief designer and thus, as he put it, Creusat is "Father of the Child."

Our discussions with a "Ms. Crusita Ramos," who said she was Dr. Creusat's secretary, likewise proved fruitless. "No," said Ms. Ramos, "I do not know what the letters in *L.U.C.I.D.* mean."

After much curious delay and, seemingly, energetic attempts to divert us, we were, however, eventually able to communicate directly with Dr. Jean-Paul Creusat through his E-mail address on the Internet. Creusat, too, at first, did not give us an answer to what we thought should have been a simple request: What do the letters in the acronym, *L.U.C.I.D.*, represent?

Finally, perhaps noting our dogged persistence, the doctor E-mailed us a message in which he claims that *L.U.C.I.D.* stands for *Logical Universal Communication Interactive Databank.* Creusat also maintains that he and Dr. Anthony Halaris are not on a government payroll, but are entrepreneurs. According to Creusat, "*L.U.C.I.D.* R&D (research and development) has been privately generated." When fully developed, *L.U.C.I.D.* will, he added, "complement and enhance the International Justice System."

I leave it to your imagination whether or not Dr. Creusat is being honestly straightforward and forthcoming. The whole thing struck me as bizarre, indeed. Here was a citizen of France, Dr. Jean-Paul Creusat, M.D., who works on the staff of *Interpol,* a European-based international police agency, and who is also somehow affiliated with the United Nations, involved with two little-known U.S. corporations, Advanced Technology Group and Birkmayer Software, designing a system for a worldwide, criminal justice computer tracking systems and control network, to be used by the CIA, FBI, *et al.* All of this he does while claiming to be independent, with funds for *L.U.C.I.D.* R&D, he says, being "privately generated."

Someone with just a half-suspicious mind might say all this smacks of the intelligence directorate of the National Security Agency (NSA).

The Ultimate Purpose of L.U.C.I.D.

While the affiliations of Creusat and Halaris remain somewhat tangled and mysterious, the ultimate purpose of *L.U.C.I.D.* is not in doubt. What *Project L.U.C.I.D.* is all about is the tracking and watching of everybody in preparing the whole world for the ironclad control of the Beast, the prophesied Antichrist. I do not accuse the lower-level technicians and professionals—men and women who help design and implement the technology which underlies this malignant project of wicked motives. Technology, in itself, is amoral. It can be used for good or evil.

Quite possibly, Professor Anthony Halaris and Dr. Jean-Paul Creusat, the men claimed to be the technological designers of *L.U.C.I.D.* systems, are blissfully unaware of the "big picture." They may not know to what malevolent purposes their technology will be dedicated. It could be that these men are no more to blame for the potential abuses of *L.U.C.I.D.* than was Albert Einstein for the employment of nuclear weapons. Einstein, in formulating his Theory of Relativity and other mathematical and physics concepts, unwittingly provided important keys to the later development and employment of the heinously deadly atom bomb.

It is the hidden chiefs at the National Security Agency, their underlings in the know, and especially their superiors, the Inner Circle of the Illuminati, whom we can rightly brand as the culprits. It is they who have conceived this colossal project and will finalize and set it into motion. If they do not repent, these men will be found guilty on Judgment Day for unspeakable crimes and treachery against God and man.

What Federal Agencies are Involved in Project L.U.C.I.D.?

In 1945, under President Harry S. Truman, a 33° Mason, a national security apparatus began to take shape. The arms of this octopus-like monster came to include the Central Intelligence Agency, the U.S. Air Force Security Service, the Naval Intelligence Service, and, of course, the National Security Agency. Over the years, the Octopus has gained monumental strength and impetus as so-called

"Internal Security" acts, "Crime Control" bills and "Anti-terrorist" legislation were passed. Today, the multiple and fattened-up arms of the Octopus envelop an incredible array of law enforcement, intelligence, and technological organizations and bureaus. Most Americans may have heard of, say, the Federal Bureau of Investigation (FBI), the Immigration and Naturalization Service (INS), the Bureau of Alcohol, Tobacco and Firearms (BATF), and the Central Intelligence Agency (CIA). And there's the Federal Communications Commission (FCC), the Food and Drug Administration (FDA), and so on. Few, also, are unaware of the ubiquitous—and *iniquitous!*—Internal Revenue Service (IRS) and the Social Security Administration (SSA). Those who have run afoul of drug laws know of the Drug Enforcement Agency (DEA).

However, it is highly unlikely that the average American—be he or she a high school dropout or a PhD—has heard of the following government agencies and systems of *control and surveillance.* Yet, it is through the networking and coordination of all these bodies that the Beast is, finally, now able to prepare for his final, great push to control and ravage humanity.

Here are just a few of the NSA-supervised interlocking groups and systems which use advanced high technology control mechanisms and comprise the Beast 666 Universal Human Control System. How many of them have *you* heard or know much of substance about?

National Reconnaissance Office (NRO)
National Law Enforcement Telecommunications System
    Projects Agency
National Crime Information Center (NCIC)
Federal Emergency Management Agency (FEMA)
Multi-Jurisdictional Task Force (MJTF)
Integrated Automated Fingerprint Identification System
    (IAFIS)
Interstate Identification Index (III)
Office of Special Investigations (OSI)
Triple I National Central Bureau (NCB)

Man and Biosphere Program (MAB)
National Strategy Information Center (NSIC)
Financial Crimes Enforcement Network (FINCEN)
Counter-Terrorist Center (CTC)
Nuclear Emergency Search Team (NEST)
Defense Information Systems Agency (DISA)
National Institute of Standards and Technology (NST)
Defense Advanced Research Projects Agency (DARPA)
Defense Intelligence Agency (DIA)
Directorate for Science and Technology (DST)
Information Infrastructure Task Force (IITF)
Air Force Systems Command (AFSC)
International Criminal Police Organization (ICPO or
    INTERPOL)
National Endowment for Democracy (NED)
National Identification Center (NIC)
National Security Council (NSC)
Computer Emergency Response Team Coordination
    Center (CERT)
Defense Message Agency (DMA)
Law Enforcement Satellite System (LESS)
Combined DNA Identification System (CDIS)

Shameless Immorality

The above is only a minute and partial list of those connected to *L.U.C.I.D.* These powerful spy and police agencies are part of our unknown American Gestapo SS establishment. No wonder Clark Matthews, a computer consultant, writer, and authority on technological control systems, recently exclaimed that, "The government continues shamelessly seeking new powers and high tech social controls that could combine the intrusiveness of George Orwell's vision of 1984 with the immorality of Lenin's liquidations of the 1920s." [5]

Under the Clinton administration, says a concerned Matthews, the nation has suffered "waves of legislation, study groups, and pilot programs, all designed to fatten federal dossiers and increase governmental control over every American."[6]

Matthews compares the many, new, spy and police government agencies, control systems, and programs akin to the plagues contained in Pandora's box. The trouble really started, he sagely observes, when Pandora opened her box and "turned them all loose at once."[7]

Now, Matthews reports, after years of government building up its "high tech American Leviathan, the plagues are all out of the box."[8]

I concur with Clark Matthews' wise analysis. The plagues are, indeed, out of the box and are threatening to infect humanity with fear and destruction. *Project L.U.C.I.D.* is taking final shape.

A Shadow Government

Other knowledgeable Americans who cherish the Constitution and its Bill of Rights and who, unlike the "dumbed-down" masses, are aware of the hideous, federal and global Behemoth now slouching toward us, are expressing their profound concern. In *Perceptions* magazine, Dr. Richard J. Boylan listed a number of "secret, often dangerous and hugely expensive agencies, projects, and groups of the three branches" of what he calls our present "Shadow Government."[9]

It is, said Boylan, "a largely hidden, second government in the country, which parallels the first (legal) government." Their activities, he noted, "are completely unknown to the average taxpayer funding them."[10]

Mysterious "National Identification Center" Established

Boylan's research into the Shadow Government dovetails with that of myself and others. In late 1994, in my international newsletter, *Flashpoint*, I unmasked, for example, the establishment of a mysterious "National Identification Center." While Dr. Creusat and Dr. Halaris contend that their *L.U.C.I.D.* is a "prospective system," not fully in place, there exists voluminous evidence that *L.U.C.I.D.* will merely add the finishing touches on a Beast 666 Universal Human Control System which has already been erected and *now awaits the* full implementation of the *L.U.C.I.D.* net to grab hold of total power and wield unparalleled, monstrous control over humanity. Thus, I label the entire operation to overlay the world with this vast, satanic web of electronic evil and slavery, *Project LUCID.* It is the project the devil will use to cause all persons to worship the image of the Beast (Revelation 13).

Here is what I reported in *Flashpoint*, in 1994, about the *already established* National Identification Center:

> Is there any person naive enough to still believe that the recent spate of legislative proposals for gun control, identification cards, and other "control of the people" schemes are not part of an overall, carefully planned and crafted conspiracy? If so, what I'm about to reveal here should open the eyes of the most gullible of citizens.
>
> Unknown to the public at large and conveniently unreported in either the liberal or conservative media, the Congress and the White House have secretly colluded to build and establish a monstrosity called the *National Identification Center.* Located in Virginia, this facility will be completed, up and running in about two years. It will enable federal law enforcement and "spook" agencies to use a state-of-the-art computer system to totally control every aspect of our lives. *This is Big Brother/Big Sister Government gone wild!*
>
> The facts about the new National Identification Center are being kept bottled up for now, lest the citizenry become alarmed and rise up to demand their congressmen kill the project. But one congressman, Representative Neal Smith, from Iowa's 4th District, inadvertently released significant information about the government's unconstitutional, Gestapo scheme in his

constituent newsletter this last October 1993. Discussing the subject of handgun control (which Rep. Smith enthusiastically favors), the Congressman boasted:

> The Subcommittee on Appropriations which I chair has been actively pursuing an effective solution to this problem...*but the program we are implementing will take more time.* The solution to screening people...is to have a National Center computerized so that local law enforcement offices can instantly access information from all states. In other words, all states would supply that information to the National Center, and the National Center will have a positive identification system which will identify any applicant...

That Congressman Neal Smith's unconstitutional "final solution" to gun control and other "crime" issues—a National Identification Center—is not just a proposal, but a looming reality, was proven by this startling admission:

> *We have invested $392 million so far in such a Center,* about a four hour drive from Washington, D.C., and we hope to have it completed and equipped in about two years... We hope all states will be in the system by 1998 and will supply the information on a continuing basis...

> Meanwhile, we will continue to establish the National Identification Center *for this and other law enforcement purposes.*

Please observe: the National Identification Center will not only enable governmental controllers to track and identify gun owners, it will also be used, Smith admits, *for other law enforcement purposes.* Like what? Well, for starters, no doubt the Center will identify and keep track of resisters to the New World Order: fundamentalist Christians and patriots, enemies of the state like you and me and our loved ones.

In light of this, how profound, then, are the Bible's prophecies which warn of the beast, the Antichrist to come in the last days. His last days' government will cause all to take a mark. His police corps will register and keep track of the citizenry so that "no man might buy or sell, save he that had the mark, or the name of the beast, or the number of his name."

Is the National Identification Center, then, a fulfillment of prophecy? I believe the answer is *yes*. But, of course, it is only one component of a wider system of Antichrist control now being put in place. For example, there is also the new National Reconnaissance Office, which oversees satellite spying of the citizenry, and there is the new, Big Brother/Big Sister clipper chip, already designed and now being installed in telephones, TVs, and other consumer electronic products.

Jesus our Saviour told us of the signs to expect as His return draws nigh. He admonished us to "watch" and take note. Well, my friends, I'm watching these things closely and all I can say is, "Even so, come quickly, Lord Jesus!"

A Spider's Web of Connected Databases

It should be noted that, since my revelations in 1994, Congressman Neal Smith and his office staff refuse to answer inquiries about the National Identification Center. However, a recent article in *Federal Computer Week*, a Washington, D.C. magazine for federal employees, basically admitted the existence of this Center and its activities. In his article, "Federal Agencies Link, Share Databases," John Monroe wrote:

Law enforcement agencies across the federal government have poured money into information technology programs. According to the Government Market Services

Division, federal agencies will spent 5.5 billion dollars on law enforcement technology between 1995 and 1999...*The common link in these programs is to build an information substructure: a web of connected databases and high speed networks that will make data instantly available to federal, state, and local law enforcement officials.*

The federal government's goal is to bring random pieces of data together to get a more complete picture—what some call *intelligence.*[11]

Monroe, who, as a federal lackey, seemed to approve of this Big Brother system, went on to reveal that practically every federal agency, from the FBI to the Immigration and Naturalization Service, the Drug Enforcement Administration, the Customs Service, the Secret Service, the Justice Department and the Treasury Department— all were being linked together in a *vast, connected computer "intelligence" network.* Indeed, a coordinating command post has been set up to build this system, benignly called the *Federal Law Enforcement Wireless Users Group.*[12]

Ominously, the article in *Federal Computer Week* states that the computerized system could be used in "field operations," through handheld instruments and devices connecting by satellite with the central brains of the computer network. Equally revolting is the revelation that, "Federal agencies are extending these links to *state and local* law enforcement organizations."[13]

In other words, once *Project L.U.C.I.D.* is in place, the whole, constitutional system of our founding fathers, who wisely separated state and local police powers from federal authority, will effectively be obliterated. A Big Brother colossus will replace a rich, 200 years-plus heritage of separated police powers.

Clark Matthews, writing in *Mondo 2000*, sums up our current, precarious situation. America and the world, Matthews says, are racing wildly into the arms of a malevolent Big Brother:

Almost from the day President Clinton assumed office, it became obvious. The secret guardians of national security and public order were fully prepared to pervert the new generation of information technologies into a monstrously sophisticated, digitotalitarian police state.

The Total Surveillance State taking shape under his leadership appears to have three broad components:

• Automatic spying on all public and private communications networks.

• Automatic "profiling" of all citizens by computer: gathering all available details—health, consumer habits, political activities, etc.

• Digital identity and social control mechanisms; in particular, Smart Cards featuring ultra-dense integrated circuitry and trackable Clipper-chip encryption.

A Smart Card is literally a computer on a credit card, complete with large amounts of digital storage, and even potential wireless communications capabilities. Once Smart Cards and digital cash come into wide use, there is no doubt that this system can be designed to function with ruthless effectiveness.

The information sciences—and the touted "Information Superhighway"—are being perverted into a Total Surveillance State. This year, for example, numerous federal agencies suddenly announced virtually complete plans to restrict access to their services to Smart Cards only.[14]

A Clear and Present Danger

Matthews' analysis is keenly on target. Everything, obviously, is being orchestrated from the top. All federal agencies are being integrated into *L.U.C.I.D.* net.

These police state agencies constitute a clear and present danger, not only to the privacy and constitutional rights of Americans but to our very lives! Through the assistance of scores of new "alphabet" police agencies and systems created in recent decades, *Project L.U.C.I.D.* is taking firm root. A Hitler, a Pol Pot, or a Stalin would have loved to have had the microchips, surveillance cameras, lasers, computers, satellites, electromagnetic wave, mind control weapons, wiretap circuits, and communications gadgetry of today's Dick Tracy police state.

Dick Tracy, of course, was a good guy. But what we shall discover is that the bad guys are now in charge. They have installed in America and around the globe a comprehensive, Orwellian system that a Dick Tracy would have recognized as unconstitutional and rejected as a menace to true law and order.

For more than a quarter of a century, hidden elements in American society, working closely with foreign powers, have built up this nightmarish, octopus-like system of total human control. Now, finally, as we draw near to the dawning of the 21st century and a new millennium, the nation that has given the world so much—from the telephone to the jet and the television—can boast once more that we are planet earth's premier inventor.

We, the astute, brilliant, and ingenious Americans, have constructed the most sophisticated, revolutionary and technologically capable SS Gestapo establishment in the annals of mankind. With *Project L.U.C.I.D.* as the capstone of this unparalleled, hyper-efficient and systematized SS Gestapo establishment, surely the world will never be the same. To understand *L.U.C.I.D.* and the ultimate evil it stands for is to peer over the edge into the abyss, where man's dismal future under totalitarian rule is to be found. Carefully and prayerfully read the following chapter, which outlines the *L.U.C.I.D.* system as touted by its promoters. Read and understand, for the time, truly, is short.

TWO

No Place Left to Hide

U nder *Project L.U.C.I.D.*, the global computer network is so cunningly designed that no one could possibly escape its all seeing, all knowing, artificial intelligence. Many will no doubt seek to short-circuit the system in one way or another. Ingenious computer hackers will do their utmost to unlock the keys to its electronic, silicon brain. But it is so constructed, with so many fail-safe, layered structures, and is designed with such intricate and complex, cryptological coding, that avoidance will be impossible. *There will be no place left to hide!*

In a strange quirk of occultic fate, with his *L.U.C.I.D.* net, Lucifer is doing his pitiful best to mimic God. The Bible tells us that when the Lord returns, men shall not be able to flee His great wrath.

> And the kings of the earth, and the great men, and the rich men, and the chief captains, and the mighty men, and every bondman, and every free man, hid themselves in the dens and in the rocks of the mountains; And said to the mountains and rocks, Fall on us, and hide us from the face of him that sitteth on the throne, and from the wrath of the Lamb: For the great day of his wrath is come; and who shall be able to stand? (Revelation 6:15-17)

Lucifer, in a pale imitation of almighty God, is attempting to establish a well-ordered, closed, planetary system of human control. *Project L.U.C.I.D.* is his chosen vehicle—the system by which he will be venting his own wrath on the inhabitants of the earth.

To grasp just how expertly planned and conceived Lucifer's system is, we turn our attention to the special features of the *L.U.C.I.D.* network. Surprisingly, though much of what *L.U.C.I.D.* entails is kept under wraps, its designers, Professor Anthony Halaris and Dr. Jean-Paul Creusat, have provided us a bird's eye view of the system in two, key articles published in *Narc Officer* magazine.[1]

Narc Officer magazine is the official journal of the International Narcotic Enforcement Officers Association. The magazine is read mostly by federal agents but also by many state and local law enforcement authorities and by foreign and corporate intelligence and police interests. Thus, the publication of these articles in *Narc Officer* graphically indicates that *L.U.C.I.D.* is so far along in its development and employment that the top officials of the National Security Agency—and the elite for whom they toil—have given the O.K. for the lower-level intelligence and police bureaucrats to have this information.

How L.U.C.I.D. Works

Let us then go straight to these explanatory articles by the two authors, Creusat and Halaris, to examine what *L.U.C.I.D.* is and how it works.

First, we discover that the name, *L.U.C.I.D.*, is copyrighted. In discussing the system, Creusat and Halaris consistently include the trademark sign (©) each time the word *L.U.C.I.D.* is mentioned. The implications of their law enforcement tracking and identification system enjoying trademark protection can only be guessed at. We must conclude, however, that under existing copyright and trademark laws, no private company will be allowed in the future to use the acronym *L.U.C.I.D.* for any other system, company, or product.

L.U.C.I.D., we are told, is intended to be a *"Universal Identification System."* Its use, we are further advised, will be effective "in year 2000 and beyond."[2]

It is implied that L.U.C.I.D. will *progressively* be installed and become operational, so that its target date of completion—the year 2000—will be met.

The universal and comprehensive nature of the L.U.C.I.D. surveillance and tracking network is indicated by the authors' comment that, "L.U.C.I.D. system will be an all source fusion information center that will interface multilingual messages into a common communications network."[3]

In plain English, this means that data and information will stream into the L.U.C.I.D. computer system from "all sources"—that is, every government agency, every bureau, every bank and financial institution, every corporation, every university, every vendor and sales merchant, every police unit, every military branch, every investigator, and on and on. Thus, all information will be "fused," that is, collected, consolidated, analyzed, and acted upon, by L.U.C.I.D.

This will be the single point, the command center and global brain for the surveillance of every person on earth. It will deposit every transaction, every piece of gossip, and every bit of information available on all the 5.5 billion people who inhabit the earth.

The fact that L.U.C.I.D. "will interface multilingual messages into a common communications network" means that L.U.C.I.D. will collect and process messages from around the globe in whatever language transmitted. L.U.C.I.D. will be the New World Order's single agency for identification, tracking, spying, surveillance, and enforcement. It is to become the consolidated and unified registry for Universal Biometrics Cards issued globally to citizens and all the data contained by the cards' integrated microchips.

Most significant, all computers on earth—the entire *Information Superhighway*—will be networked into L.U.C.I.D. It will be the planet's primary, core, "common communications network," linking all other computer networks and data systems. In sum, who can doubt that

L.U.C.I.D. is slated to become the *Beast 666 Universal Human Control System.*

The Beast 666 Universal Human Control System

The beast nature of *L.U.C.I.D.* is confirmed by the statement of Creusat and Halaris in their article in *Narc Officer* magazine that the *L.U.C.I.D.* net will be the world's *"Universal Computerized Identification Clearinghouse Resource Center."*[4] Please, read this title again, all *six* words of it. Ponder and contemplate each word in the title: *Universal... Computerized...Identification...Clearinghouse...Resource... Center.* The implications and importance of *L.U.C.I.D.* are staggering!

Yet another vital clue to the earth-shattering significance of *L.U.C.I.D.* is the statement by its designers, Creusat and Halaris, that the system will implement "a secure, interactive, and instantaneous universal information system."[5] I believe *secure* means that only those authorized by Big Brother will have access to the incredible accumulation of data stored in the system. *Interactive* means that Gestapo units across the globe granted access by a special, restricted entry code will be using the system to track and control individuals and their every movement. *Instantaneous* means instant data served upon request. The system is described by Creusat and Halaris as providing "24 hour service, 7 days a week."[6]

The global scope of *L.U.C.I.D.* is signified by the statement that the system will receive and digest messages and information requests "from developing as well as industrialized countries." It is to be a "universal point of contact," we are told. It will centralize and contain input and data on individuals obtained from: "The networks of federal, state, and local government agencies; public and private nonprofit organizations; NCIC (nationwide law enforcement computer system); NCB-Interpol; Triple I; and the Department of Justice, and will be the essential communications link between national and international law enforcement agencies and...participating countries' Department of State and Department of Justice."[7]

In other words, this means the end of American sovereignty. We can, of course, as a consequence, kiss the Tenth Amendment to the U.S. Constitution goodbye. Now, it's "Hello world, goodbye U.S.A.!"

Tracking "Alias Criminals"

We are further advised that *L.U.C.I.D.* will facilitate—that is, make possible—"non-criminal justice background checks and tracking of positive identification request for alias criminals."[8]

What is implied by "alias criminals?" The authors give numerous examples of circumstances in which the system will be used to track so-called "alias criminals." Included is data necessary for government personnel—bureaucrats, investigators, regulators, police, and spies—to make decisions in such matters and areas as:

* Employment
* Administrative
* Immigration Status
* Licensing
* Judicial
* Investigative
* Prosecutorial
* Custodial
* Firearms Purchase

In other words, *L.U.C.I.D.* will control the entire gamut of human activity, from jobs and licenses of all kinds to court hearings and indictments, custody of children, and permits to own and/or carry a firearm. Massive quantities of intelligence and personal information will be acquired, stored, and accessed on the *L.U.C.I.D.* net.

The demented brains who want to cram *L.U.C.I.D.* down our throats are making sure that its electronic tentacles are able to race along the entire Information Superhighway, searching for juicy gossip and data on our personal lives and fortunes. Thus, we read that L.U.C.I.D. will "support, search, and update data...from the networks of federal, state and local government agencies; public and private nonprofit organizations;" and so on.[9] It will replace all other "Smart Cards" in existence.

The magnitude of this computerized endeavor boggles the imagination. Detailed dossiers are to be established and maintained on 5.5 billion people in some 200 countries around the world. It is reported that, in fiscal year (FY) 1994, just one American government computer system alone, the *National Crime Information Center (NCIC)*, processed over 506 million transactions. It is simply incalculable how many transactions will be processed under L.U.C.I.D., but the total figure should be in the *trillions*. This is virtually total control over the human population. The adage that information translates into *power* will certainly be proven correct when this heinous, intrusive system is operating at its full capacity, sometime before the advent of the 21st century.

Gateway to the Beast: The Universal Biometrics Card

It is through the *Universal Biometrics (I.D.) Card*, that the Beast 666 Universal Human Control System is to achieve its ultimate power and authority over the world's populations. According to the L.U.C.I.D. designers, all of the system's computer technology, hardware and software capability are being prepared to fit into "the framework of the future Universal Biometrics Card Model." The L.U.C.I.D. card will be a "Smart Card:" a credit-card sized I.D. made of plastic with a *translucent* microchip computer embedded in it. The Universal Biometrics Card (UBC) will be self-contained, with the built-in computer chip being *reprogrammable*.[10] In other words, at hundreds of thousands of scanner centers and sites across America and the globe, Big Brother's agents can insert your UBC Smart Card, linking it up with the *Master Computer* at headquarters—in Ft. Meade, Maryland or wherever.

Then, new or revised information can be downloaded into your card, instantly updating your "computer on-board," I.D. card with all the spy and intelligence information they have more recently dug up on you.

Meanwhile, police and other government agents anywhere in the world are able to request and receive "an instantaneous readout of individualized updated data." The computer I.D. card, the designers boast, "will not only store more than five gigabytes of individualized data, but will also be interactively read through a multilingual, transcriptor/translator, computerized cipher via a scanner reader into portable and/or fixed equipment units."[11]

This is the dark and dreadful future of high tech control awaiting each of us when what the designers proudly term the "Universal Computerized Identification Clearinghouse Resource Center" via *L.U.C.I.D.* net is implemented. It will mean the end of human freedom and dignity. And remember, they say it will all be in place and humming along Big Brother's Information Super-highway by the year 2000.

The Eyes Have It—And So Do the Fingers, and the Voice...and...

To make sure they've got you identified, and targeted, and can constantly keep track of your whereabouts and activities, the *L.U.C.I.D.* system will employ a comprehensive array of "biometrics."

Essentially, biometrics means the "measurement of biological factors." Science has for years been tremendously busy researching means of identifying a person by measuring and recording his or her *physical characteristics*. Sophisticated sensors are now capable of identifying you by the shape of your hand, foot, or head. They can measure and identify the iris of your eye and the topography of your fingerprint. There is also your blood type and your unique DNA code. Machines have also been invented that can identify you by your distinctive voice.

In a recent issue of the excellent, prophetic newspaper, *The Omega Times*, published by New Zealand author and evangelist Barry Smith, editor John Koutsimanis explained how, today, biometrics are finding common use by government and industry to identify individuals:

> Biometrics may sound a little like a company which sells skin care products, but it isn't. It is the word used to describe identification by human characteristics.
>
> Listed below are some ways that biometrics are already in use around the world. There is no doubt that biometrics technology will be standardized globally in the near future.
>
> **a:** The backs of ATMs are controlled by fingerprint biometrics. When bank personnel are dispatched to a machine, the authorized person's fingerprints are downloaded on the computer to give access to the person based on positive identification.
>
> **b:** The San Francisco International Airport has more than 80 hand geometry machines which identify the people who work there and allows them access.
>
> **c:** Los Angeles County Welfare System uses automated fingerprint searches to make sure that people are not double dipping into welfare benefits. This service has also been extended into other states.
>
> **d:** The Colombian Government has installed hand geometry machines by every seat in the Senate and House of Representatives to ensure that when representatives vote on legislation it is really them.
>
> **e:** Some state and local governments in developed countries use voice verification to identify low-risk

offenders who are confined to their homes. The computer calls at random times of the day.

f: Russia has begun using hand geometry and fingerprint verification on the Card Based Bank Accounts. With crime running wild there, it is important that the person carrying the card be identified with more than just a PIN number.

g: The Lotus Corporation has a day care centre for its employees. If the children are not feeling well, or if they don't go to school, Lotus Corp. employees bring them to the day care centre and have their hand geometry recorded. When time comes for picking up the child, the parent must be verified by re-checking their hand geometry.

h: ATM transactions for pension payments of the First National Bank of South Africa, which operates a mobile ATM service to 48,000 clients, need to have fingerprint verification.

i: The world's immigration authorities have realized that one of the easiest ways to reduce lines at major airports is to process frequent international travellers via an automated system. These travellers are given a Smartcard and, along with their hand geometry and fingerprint verification, they are processed quickly.

The above are only a handful of examples of identification by human characteristics. The world will soon be filled with this kind of technology, and cheating the law will become almost obsolete.

The downside to all of this is the fact that no matter where you go, you can always be tracked down via this multi-web of modern technology.[12]

In their article in *Narc Officer, L.U.C.I.D.* planners Dr. Jean-

Paul Creusat and Dr. Anthony Halaris outline the types of biometric information that will be acquired from people to be programmed on their individual Universal Biometrics Card as a means of identification:

> The research and development of *L.U.C.I.D.* System will demonstrate its feasibility and practicality...The design will transmit encrypted (coded) data through *L.U.C.I.D.* Net Information Infrastructure from distant biometrics sensors and/or biometric cards sensors...

> All of these methods have been developed through the use of Artificial Intelligence (AI) software, described in 1992 by R. L. Sherman in his article entitled "Biometric Futures" in *Computers and Security.* The technology will provide methods for positive identification, although observing current civil rights and civil liberties legislative guidelines, by recording human features such as photos, fingerprints, footprints, iris scans, textual data...DNA genotyping, and Human Leukocyte Antigen data, at milestones in an individual's life. These milestone data updates, via non-invasive devices, will involve only a touch of a sensor for fingerprinting, footprinting and for iris scan by a computerized pen-like camera fiber-optic (done simply by having a subject stand in front of the camera).

> Independent tests conducted by Sandia National Laboratories, New Mexico, have verified that reliable fingerprint and iris scan systems are now available for research and other uses. Permanent digitized templates will correspond to fingerprints, footprints, and iris scans. Facial photograph digitized templates, only, will be updated and stamped during periodic milestones.[13]

According to Creusat and Halaris, the following identification techniques will be secured in the memory of the "L.U.C.I.D. System Universal Biometrics Card" as digitized templates. The words and explanations are theirs:

...DNA genotyping and Human Leukocyte Antigen will be available and represent excellent technologies for determining probable identity...DNA genotyping is the process of establishing probable individual identity through scientific analysis of DNA contained in some human cellular material. Human Leukocyte Antigen tests can establish probable individual identity through scientific analysis of hereditary protein material.

Iris scan technology is a new, non-intrusive personal identifier. The Greek word iris means *"a rainbow."* It refers to the round colored part, the pigmented membrane surrounding the pupil of the eye, having muscles that adjust the size of the pupil to regulate the amount of light entering the eye. Every iris has a unique, stable, and highly detailed texture. Connecticut ophthalmologists Dr. Leonard Flom and Dr. Aran Safir patented the concept of using the iris for personal identification. Clearly visible iris features include striations, pits, rings, freckles, contraction furrows, coronas, collagenous fibers and filaments. As a whole, these diverse sources of angular and radial variation form a unique pattern. Because the iris is an internal part of the eye, it is protected from the exterior environment. Surgical alteration of the iris cannot be accomplished without a permanent impairment of vision. Also, the iris and the pupil have an automatic physiological response to light variations. The irises of identical twins are different, and even more interesting, each iris of an individual is unique. These factors all contribute to the effectiveness of the iris as the most reliable form to ascertain an individual's identity when the iris is exposed to distant public biometrics sensors. Software and hardware have been developed and tested for the iris scan. Iris detection and analysis require about one-fourth of a second. A 256-byte image or Iriscode is analyzed in about a tenth of a second. The software compares up to 4,000 complete Iriscodes per second with an indicated error rate of one in 131,000. L.U.C.I.D.

POPULAR SCIENCE OCTOBER 1994 • **49**

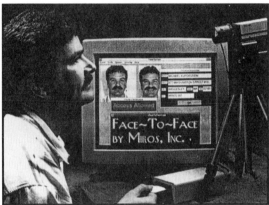

Face-To-Face uses a video camera to match a person's face with a stored image on an electronic ID card.

like human brains, have the ability to "learn" from experience.

An experimental system at Auburn University uses facial images made up of 65,536 pixels. The procedure first locates the "corners" of a photographic profile defined by critical points on the nose, lips, and chin. The computer then uses fuzzy logic and neural networking to create a ten-dimensional "feature vector" of the face. A similar project at the Massachusetts Institute of Technology uses gestalt-type images called *eigenfaces*, which are based on more

I M A G I N G

COMPUTERS WITH A MEMORY FOR FACES

You may never have thought of your face as thousands of points of light, but that's the way a com-

DNA databanks dot U.S.

Will they endanger individual privacy?

Knight-Ridder Newspapers

WASHINGTON — Thanks to the O.J. Simpson case, just about everyone knows a substance called DNA can identify criminal suspects with unusual accuracy.

What most people don't know is that a nationwide system of DNA databanks is rapidly being built. It already contains blood samples from millions of Americans, whether or not they have been involved in a crime.

Someday, these growing collections might cover every citizen, helping not only to solve murders but also to find missing children, identify plane crash victims or free

an innocent man on death row.

However, some scientists, doctors and lawyers fear these genetic fingerprints pose an unprecedented threat to individual privacy.

The idea that there will be a huge databank of genetic information on millions of people is repulsive," James Watson, who won a Nobel Prize for his pathbreaking work on DNA, told a congressional hearing in 1991.

DNA, the string of genes coiled in each of your cells, can be retrieved from blood spots, such as those found on Simpson's Bronco, from saliva and from other bodily fluids. Each person's DNA is unique, often making it a better tool for identification than conventional fingerprints, teeth or notoriously unreliable eyewitnesses.

DNA samples are currently being gathered from three major sources:

newborn babies, military recruits and convicted felons. Private research laboratories, biotechnology companies, fertilization clinics and some health insurance companies are also saving human DNA.

Some states are considering laws that would even collect DNA from people involved in minor offenses.

There are no national laws governing this growing accumulation of DNA samples. A bill that would have regulated DNA data died when Congress adjourned.

"DNA profiling poses a special risk of invasion of privacy concerning personal and medical traits," the National Research Council, a high level scientific advisory committee, declared in 1992. "DNA information could lead to discrimination by insurance companies, employers or others against people with particular traits."

3 major sources

The three major sources of DNA databanks are:
 • **Babies:** Since the 1960s, blood has been taken from newborn children as part of mandatory state screening programs for hereditary diseases such as mental retardation, cystic fibrosis, muscular dystrophy and sickle cell anemia.

Existing, upcoming

The following 19 states either maintain DNA databanks or have given permission to maintain such databanks:

Arizona
California
Colorado
Florida
Georgia
Hawaii
Illinois
Iowa
Kansas
Kentucky
Michigan
Minnesota
Missouri
Nevada
Oregon
South Dakota
Tennessee
Virginia
Washington

Iowa will start DNA databank when testing begins in July

By Rick Smith
Gazette staff writer

Iowa has not begun to build a DNA databank, though state law was granted the ... the rules have been adopted. They go into effect when the DCI announces publicly it is ready to begin testing.

Faces can now be digitized and stored in computer databanks. Meanwhile, DNA databanks are rapidly being built across America.

An eyeball on security

■ Future automatic teller machines might include iris-scanning identification system

BY LINDA A. JOHNSON
Associated Press

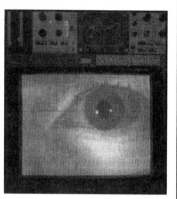

Mike Derer/AP

Sensar hopes to make personal identification numbers and ATM cards obsolete with its IrisIdent system, which verifies identity by scanning the iris.

PRINCETON, N.J. — Imagine stepping up to an automatic teller machine that knows who you are just by eyeballing you.

In just a few blinks of your eye, a computer system verifies your identity with a hidden camera that scans the 400-some identifying features of your iris and matches them to a huge database. No match, no transaction.

How iris scanning works. **D2**

Sounds like science fiction? Sensar Inc. is hoping its patented IrisIdent system will soon become a very real part of people's lives, making personal identification numbers and ATM cards obsolete

such as the FBI and CIA, said Kevin B. McQuade, the company's vice president for strategic business development.

Huntington Bancshares Inc. of Columbus, Ohio, plans to be an early test site, trying IrisIdent at a handful of ATMs in Ohio late this year.

"I suspect that there will be a significant number of institutions that will find this attractive," says Huntington's chief technology officer, John Voss. "I don't know that

NEW YORK POST. MONDAY, MAY 20, 1996   17

BANKS WILL SOON SEE POSITIVE EYE-D

By ROBERT HARDT Jr.

Iris scan foils scams

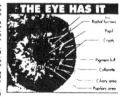

Eye irises, which are unique to each person, will soon be used for positive identification at ATMs.

L.U.C.I.D. net will take advantage of incredible, new "iris-scan" technologies.

System has been designed to ensure a comfortable and non-physical contact identification through use of an iris scan.

The Footprint of newborns is a reliable, expeditious and cost-efficient method for establishing personal identity. In the November 1994, publication of the *FBI Law Enforcement Bulletin*, Special Agent Michael E. Stapleton advocated in his article, "Best Foot Forward," the justification of infant footprints for personal identification. The clear friction ridge minutiae recordings are an electronic easy method of footprinting the ball of the newborn foot because this area contains sufficient ridge detail to make an identification. In addition, including the fingerprinting of the mother on the infant's footprint document links the child to the mother within two hours of birth, preferably before the infant is removed from the delivery room, eliminating any doubt of parentage. This method is supported by the FBI and the National Center for Missing and Exploited Children in their infant abduction prevention guidelines issued to medical facilities nationwide.

The Fingerprint is a physical characteristic currently available throughout various database programs kept at the NCIC and nonprofit organizations such as the National Fingerprint Program for Child Identification located at the University of Illinois at Chicago, Illinois. Electronic fingerprinting will be the biometrics technology used in the L.U.C.I.D. System as a convenient and practical way to ascertain an individual's identity.[14]

They're Watching You Every Minute

If you think the new Universal Biometrics Card will merely be a convenient tool you and I use to have banks, food and department stores, and others verify we are who we say we are, you're sadly mistaken. Remember, *L.U.C.I.D.'s* designers, Creusat and Halaris, have told us the system will be used to acquire information and data "from *distant* biometrics sensors and/or biometrics cards sensors."

This is our wake-up call, telling us that the gory eyes and long, sucking tentacles of the electronic, octopus beast will literally be everywhere. You and I are to be watched, measured, evaluated, and watched again. How? Via *distant* surveillance, monitoring, and tracking sensors, no doubt hidden in locations and sites we could not possibly envision.

In Vietnam, sensors were dropped from U.S. aircraft along the Ho Chi Minh trail and other transportation routes taken by North Vietnamese military forces pushing into South Vietnam. These sensors detected people who came into close proximity and sent back the messages to computers at U.S. military installations. The process resulted in fighter and bomber aircraft being dispatched to rain down fire and destruction on unwitting victims.

Today, biometrics sensors are being "seeded" across the United States, Canada, Europe, and in many other countries. These sensors/devices are constantly sending digitized messages to the NSA and its subsidiary police and spy organizations. Such a massive, centralized collecting and processing of untold trillions of bits of information daily by sophisticated, computerized sensors is unprecedented. It means the death knell for privacy of the people and the demise of our long cherished constitutional rights.

A conspiratorial elite who would order this Gestapo beast system into operation must truly despise the Bill of Rights, and especially the Fourth Amendment to the U.S. Constitution, intended to preserve the right of American citizens to be safe, secure, and protected against unreasonable searches and seizures.

But *L.U.C.I.D.*, regardless of the protests of its makers and designers, is a killer of the Fourth Amendment, not to mention the First Amendment, which guarantees our right of free speech. After all, with its legions of sensors, *L.U.C.I.D.* promises to watch, search, snoop, and deprive us all of privacy, "24 hours a day, 7 days a week."

Examples abound of interlinking and computer-connected biometrics systems being built everywhere. The technological capability is exploding. We are fast becoming "lucid;" that is, clear and transparent, to government agents and agencies. Again, I emphasize, there is now *nowhere* to hide.

They'll Have Your Face Digitized

Consider, for example, a technology called *"Face Recognition."* *Popular Science* magazine reports that, "New software and accessories are making it possible for computers to digitize, analyze, and identify faces...such identification might provide an electronic key..." The magazine goes on to explain that artificial intelligence (AI) and a new method called "fuzzy logic" now exists to give computers a capacity for facial recognition on a par with the human brain.[15]

Meanwhile, *Face-to-Face,* a $25,000 machine from Miros, Inc. of Wellesley Massachusetts, uses computers and Microsoft *(Windows)* software to create a digital cutout of a person's face and match it with a previously taken picture stored in a database or an I.D. card. The system works even if you attempt to fool it by wearing glasses or makeup. Now, since *L.U.C.I.D.* is also based on Microsoft Corporation's *Windows* software, we gain a clue to how this capability is going to be used.

Intelligent Video, a system developed by Integrated Systems, Inc. of Norcross, Georgia, is even more spectacular. It is programmed to look not only for facial characteristics, but also *body language* unique to the individual being tracked and monitored. Thousands of these video cameras distantly controlled by computer can be covertly installed in buildings and on streets to watch for specific people. When a "match" is made, the computer immediately notifies authorities. So wherever we go, we are to be watched and our movements reported to Big Brother's data reporting agency.

In places like Singapore, in Asia, and in Great Britain,

these intelligent camera systems are already in operation—
300,000 in Britain alone! These nations are being turned
into video-monitored bird cages. But instead of birds, it is
men and women who are trapped inside electronic cages.

Simon Davies, Director-General of the Washington,
D.C.-based watchdog group, Privacy International, reported
recently that the new video computer devices with facial
recognition technology were installed for the '96 Olympics
in Atlanta, Georgia. How many realized that, as they
watched these sporting events, they, too, were being
watched?[16]

Satellites Watching Us

Satellite technology is paramount in the brave, new
technetronic world being built for our prison-like lifestyles.
When the Cold War ended in 1990 (or so we were told!),
a naive public thought our military surveillance satellites
would be mothballed. After all, tens of billions of defense
dollars were being spent annually to launch and maintain
an intensive global surveillance capability. Not so. The
Illumined Ones have always had big, big plans for satellite
tattletalers.

Satellite cameras are so advanced that, from space,
they can take recognizable 35mm-type images of golf balls
on earth below. They can tell whether a person has long
hair or is bald. Nowhere on earth is there any privacy
because of these spy-in-the-sky invaders.

Orbiting satellites are also linked with earth-based
implantable biochips and microchip sensors and transmitters. When you carry your brand new Universal
Biometrics Card (UBC) in your wallet or purse, a satellite
can be tracking your movements. They are able to do so
thanks to a system of 24 global positioning satellites (GPS)
orbiting the earth at all times.[17] Admittedly, you and I
could rebel, junking the UBC plastic computer card and
refusing to carry it on our person. But then, we may not
be able to buy or sell without it. We can't operate an

automobile, or get a job. We won't be able to cash a check or obtain medical care.

This is bad enough, but in just a few more years, if Big Brother's Plan succeeds, we'll all have the translucent biochip cards imbedded *under our skin!* The Universal Biometrics Card will be an alien part of our very bodies. We really *won't* be able to leave home without it.

In the early 1990s, our huge, *Star Wars* fleet of orbiting spy satellites, complete with their Top Secret NASA missions and their links to ground-based sensors and to the developing, computer, personal spy net, fell under the authority of a newly organized Gestapo organization called the *National Reconnaissance Office.* A gargantuan spy facility, this complex has been built outside the Washington, D.C. metroplex. The price tag was in the $400 million range. All this at a time when the Russians are said to be a faded, virtually nonexistent threat and the military justification for this system is nil. Of course, containment of the Russians and other foreign enemies, really, never was the reason for our global-watching space vehicles. The real reason all along has been to set up the capability for the soon coming Beast 666 Universal Human Control System.

How many Americans have even the vaguest notion that so-called "Smart Highway" surveillance cameras are now in operation on major highways, roads, and bridges? More frightening are alarming reports that the newer, "interactive" television sets are being fitted with hidden, miniaturized cameras and microchips to permit your voice and image to be transmitted back to the watchers at Big Brother's data reporting agency.

The Eyes Have It

Newer and better ways to spy on and keep track of us are constantly being found. Corporations know there are huge profits to be made from selling government and industry these human control systems.

In *The New York Post* recently was a prime example of how close we are to being required to submit to the new *Iris Scan* technology. The article, cutely titled, "Banks Will Soon See Positive Eye-D," said, "It seems like it's right out of a James Bond movie." The iris of the customer's eye is scanned and enters the database. After that, he or she will never need re-scanning. This will be a *permanent* means of identification.[18]

"When the customer later approaches a cash machine," we are informed, "a camera that takes five pictures a second would hone in on his eye." The iris image can be surveyed from three feet away at present. But future advances will enable the iris to be checked from across a room or street. "In initial tests of the machine's accuracy," *The New York Post* reports, "it correctly matched 1,994 out of 1,995 study participants."[19]

DNA Databanks Set Up

So the iris-scanning devices are here, now! And remember: The Universal Biometrics Card also contains the individual's DNA. How close are we to universally implementing this police state technique to identify and track the citizenry? Well, several years ago, in 1994, a feature story by the Knight-Ridder news syndicate ran in scores of newspapers across the U.S.A. It was entitled, "DNA Databanks Dot U.S." The news story unearthed the mind-boggling report that the DNA databanks are already being built and put into operation. Here's a portion of what was revealed:

> Thanks to the O. J. Simpson case, just about everyone knows a substance called DNA can identify criminal suspects with unusual accuracy.

> What most people don't know is that a nationwide system of DNA databanks is rapidly being built. It already contains blood samples from millions of Americans, *whether or not* they have been involved in a

crime...Someday, these growing collections might cover
every citizen...

However, some scientists, doctors, and lawyers fear these
genetic fingerprints pose an unprecedented threat to
individual privacy. "The idea that there will be a huge
databank of genetic information on millions of people is
repulsive," James Watson, who won a Noble Prize for his
pathbreaking work on DNA, told a congressional hearing
in 1991...

The three major sources of DNA databanks are:

• **Babies:** Since the 1960s, blood has been taken from
newborn children as part of mandatory state screening
programs for hereditary diseases such as mental
retardation, cystic fibrosis, muscular dystrophy and
sickle cell anemia.

• **Military:** Since June 1992, blood and saliva samples
have been collected from every recruit. Almost 700,000
samples—known informally as "DNA dog tags"—are
already on file. Thousands more are received daily at
the Defense Department's DNA Repository.

• **Criminals:** Since 1991, the FBI has been building a
national catalog of DNA samples collected by state
and local law enforcement agencies. About half the
states have set up databases, which are being linked
into the national network known as CODIS (Combined
DNA Identification System).[20]

Do you think it mere chance that the government has,
for some years now, been furiously collecting DNA
samples? Is it by accident that, since 1991, the FBI has
been building a "national catalog of DNA samples," and
that the government has set up a national DNA database
network "known as *CODIS (Combined DNA Identification
System)?*"[21]

Is it also by accident that the government, for years, has been energetically plotting out and designing an escape-proof Universal Biometrics Card system that uses the individual's unique DNA code as an identification tool? And finally, is it by accident that the nationwide CODIS network of DNA samples is automatically linked with the *L.U.C.I.D.* net?

Is this not part of the great, prophetically revealed *Master Plan* to construct a Luciferian identification control system so that "no man might buy or sell, save he that had the mark, or the name of the beast, or the number of his name?"

SS Gestapo-Like Innovations

When we combine these new, SS Gestapo-like innovations with the federal government's recent successes in policing the *internet* and dominating its on-line message bulletin board systems, we begin to realize the monumental changes occurring in American society.

Thus, Privacy International's Simon Davies points out that because of the boom in surveillance technologies, "An intimacy without parallel will mean that areas of life traditionally considered private, will be comprehensively revealed."[22]

"Surveillance technology," Davies adds, "will enjoy a fast track into all areas of our lives."[23]

Davies is speaking only of the technological capability of government to intrude into our private lives with its spy and surveillance wizardry. But *Project L.U.C.I.D.* is designed to take chilling advantage of the entire range of technology which *already* exists. As Dr. Antony Sutton, author and former fellow of the Hoover Institution, emphasizes:

> The identification techniques used by *L.U.C.I.D.* are already developed and, whatever its designers say, are extraordinarily invasive of personal liberties.[24]

What's more, the system will become even more all-powerful as newer, more precise and more dictatorially efficient, hideous technologies are developed. It was the Englishman, A. K. Chesterton, who once declared the existence of a conspiracy so immense and so diabolical that the end result would be the imprisonment of mankind and a One World tyranny. In his *The New Unhappy Lords: An Exposure of Power Politics*, he declared:

> I claim the existence of a conspiracy for the destruction of the Western World as the prelude for shepherding mankind into a sheep's pen run as a prelude to One World tyranny.[25]

How astute and prophetic were the words of Chesterton. *Project L.U.C.I.D.* does, in fact, seem to provide the means for the "shepherding of mankind into a sheep's pen run." And, as the Bible (Revelation 13) forewarned, it is a numbering, identification, and marking system like *L.U.C.I.D.* that was prophesied to be the "prelude to One World tyranny" under the direction of the Antichrist, 666.

THREE

The New MARK Card— "Don't Leave Home Without It!"

N ational Citizen I.D. is Proposed" read the headline in *USA Today*. Reporting from Washington, D.C., news reporter Maria Puente informed readers that, "All U.S. citizens and legal immigrants would receive the equivalent of a national I.D. card under an expected proposal to Congress by the Commission on Immigration Reform, chaired by former Democrat Congresswoman Barbara Jordan."[1]

This announcement of a pending national I.D. card raised hackles among patriotic Americans. A veritable firestorm of protest flooded congressional phone and fax lines. Stunned by the negative response, the Jordan Commission backtracked, announcing that the I.D. card will be delayed *for now*. Instead, the Commission proposes that *"a national data base"* be established. In effect, this would be a Big Brother/Big Sister computer system with every citizen's primary data entered therein.

The Master Plan

But, watch out! The federals have not given up on their idea of a national I.D. card. They need this to control the citizen peons. Their master plan calls, first, for a photographic, bar coded, biometrics I.D. card of every man, woman, and child, complete with a built-in computer chip dossier and file. The I.D. cards of so-called "Enemies of the State" (yes, friends, you and me!) will be so designated.

However, once the populace gets used to their spiffy new I.D. cards and sees how simple it is to buy, sell, and apply for a job or a loan with it, the federals will advance to Step 2 of "The Plan."

Under Step 2, the government will inform the duped masses that the Smart I.D. Card is no longer useful. In fact, the bureaucrats will lament, the card is an onerous burden. It takes up room in one's wallet or purse. It can be lost or stolen. Wouldn't it be easier and more convenient and efficient for us to just insert a tiny microchip in the forehead or right hand of everyone? Then you really cannot "leave home without it!"

Mexico's I.D. Card—A CIA Project?

The government, therefore, will first try to convince us that we *need* the national I.D. card. To accomplish this propaganda feat, a score of experimental tests are underway. In 1994, down in Mexico, the American CIA and their Mexican NAFTA partners issued citizens the new, computerized "Voter's Smart Card." The cards were developed jointly by U.S. multinational corporations Polaroid, IBM, Booz-Allen and Hamilton, and Oracle (a California software company). The corrupt Mexican government spent $730 million to deliver the cards to that nation's 46 million voters. The money came, I believe, from a secret, CIA "spook" banking account.

Now, if you believe that this I.D. card, Mexico's first national identification system, guarantees honest, free elections down Mexico way, I have this great bridge, located in Louisiana's swamplands, that I'd like to sell you at a bargain price.

While the CIA and the Mexicanos are using the citizenry down South for experimental purposes, here in the good old U.S.A., the government department that Bill Clinton truly loathes—the Department of Defense—is assisting the administration in conducting yet another Big Brother/Big Sister test. This time, our nation's soldiers are unwittingly being used as psychological guinea pigs.

These troops are enrolled in a program for what is revealingly being called the *MARC*. Yes, you read it correctly. The Department of Defense (DOD) is issuing its new MARC. They don't even describe it as a "card." Just the MARC.

According to the DOD, the term MARC is an acronym for *Multi-Technology Automated Reader Card (M A R C)*. We are told that, "The MARC has a standard bar code, a magnetic stripe, embossed data, a digital photograph and an Integrated Circuit (IC) computer chip." It contains a massive array of information and is used by the carrier to make purchases and store his or her complete military and healthcare records file.

The Purpose is Control

The national I.D. card is being promoted to us as a benefit—a convenience. Don't believe it. The government's real purpose is *control*. A central database and a computer I.D. card will ensure minute control of the citizenry by instilling fear in peoples' hearts. As Rupert Butler wrote in his book, *An Illustrated History of the Gestapo*, under Nazism, "All German citizens had to carry identification and could be stopped at any time by either civilian or military police."[2]

The Communist police states followed the same pattern as the Nazis. All tyrannical governments are consumed with the same obsessive urge to control their citizenry with I.D. cards and national registries. Don McAlvany, in his *The McAlvany Intelligence Advisor*, writes:

> In all communist countries, the citizens (or slaves) must carry identification papers on their person at all times and must be ready to present their papers to communist

authorities at *all* times—at border check points, at train or bus stations, airports, road blocks, etc. Every such citizen fears the ominous words "show me your papers."

But those papers were not computerized. The new National Identification Card being pushed by the Clintonistas will ultimately be a computerized smartcard that can carry hundreds of pages of data (up to 2000 pages) on each American citizen.

The Establishment/New World Order crowd and their Clintonista employees are very close to locking the chains on all Americans via a high tech National Identification Card linked to government databases that will destroy 100% of all Americans' privacy and enable the government to control virtually all aspects of our lives.[3]

To vividly illustrate the truth of what Don McAlvany is saying, we have the bloody example of what happened in Rwanda, the country in Africa, where, in 1995, up to a million men, women, and children were bludgeoned, shot, and hacked to death in mass killings by military forces and by rival, tribal groups. Victims were picked out because of the information reported on their *mandatory* I.D. Cards. As reported in the *San Francisco Chronicle:*

Rwanda will no longer distinguish between Hutus and Tutsis when it issues new identity cards, ending a practice that helped Hutu militiamen to select their victims in last year's genocide, officials said yesterday.

They said residency cards are being issued this week in Kigali and they will be distributed in the rest of Rwanda later.

During last year's genocide, Hutu militiamen demanded the identity cards of civilians they stopped. If they were listed as members of the Tutsi minority, they were hacked to death or shot.[4]

Setting Up of the Mark of the Beast

Intelligence analyst C. B. Baker believes that what is planned is nothing less than "the setting up of the 666 mark of the beast system." Commenting on a report in *The Washington Times* newspaper that, under the government scheme, everyone will carry "Smart (I.D.) Cards," coded with personal information, Baker warns:

> The universal requirement that everybody carry such "Smart Cards," will help the federal government create a Marxist Satanic dictatorship, and signals End Times events predicted in Revelation 13:16-18. "And he causeth all, both small and great, rich and poor, free and bond, to receive a mark in their right hand, or in their foreheads: And that no man might buy or sell, save he that had the mark, or the name of the beast, or the number of his name"—666.[5]

It is interesting that Baker mentions the prophetic forecast found in the book of Revelation of a universal identification system to be mandated for the *whole world*. At the time the Apostle John was given this prophetic vision, Rome ruled western civilization. In that era, to identify their soldiers and slaves, the Roman authorities issued them a piece of a Mosaic. The Mosaic, called "tesserea," was a form of I.D. How fascinating that this very same term, *tesserea*, has been suggested by the National Security Agency and Defense Intelligence Agency as the code name for the proposed, new citizens' I.D. card!

Meanwhile, the plan to introduce the tesserea card and require its use universally is known as *Project Mosaic*. As if this were not enough to cause those of us with discernment to understand the ominous intentions of our controllers, the actual chip that will go into the I.D. cards is being called the *Capstone*.

This use of the term *Capstone* dredges up two, related objectives of the plan of today's SS establishment to control us with computerized I.D. chips. First, the computerized system will serve as the *capstone* of the New World Order, also called the New Civilization. Second, the separation now illustrated on our U.S. one dollar bill between the New World Order *(Novus Ordo Seclorum)* pyramid and the capstone above it, picturing the all seeing eye of Lucifer, the sun god of light, will be ended.

The capstone is descending and will be joined to the pyramid by the Illuminati's Masonic builders. The Illuminati's conspiracy of the ages will be culminated with *L.U.C.I.D.* I.D. net providing the logical, ultimate means of shackling the peoples of the world.

The Hunger to Control Us

What other conclusion can we come to than that the New World Order's insatiable hunger to fulfill Satan's conspiracy of the ages is fueling the current campaign to issue I.D. cards to every living being on earth? For years now, this hunger to control the masses—almost a bloodlust—has built up in the polluted minds of bureaucrats. Martin Anderson, a senior advisor on the President's Economic Policy Advisory Board during the Reagan administration, recently described this curiously oppressive, bureaucratic mind-set:

> The smart card is an open, engraved invitation to a national identity card. In the early 1980s when I worked in the West Wing of the White House as President Reagan's domestic policy adviser, I was surprised by the ardent desire of government bureaucrats, many of them Reagan appointees, for a national identity card.
>
> Brushing aside any concerns about personal privacy, a powerful array of government agencies—the Immigration and Naturalization Service, the State Department, the FBI, the IRS, the CIA—each with its own special reasons, lusted after a law to force every American to carry a national identity card. Such a law was within a whisker

of being endorsed by Reagan's Cabinet in July 1981 and was stopped only when President Reagan personally vetoed the idea on the grounds it was a massive invasion of privacy.

The idea of a national identity card, with a new name, has risen once again from the graveyard of bad policy ideas, more powerful and virulent than ever. Unless it is stopped quickly we may live to see the end of privacy in the United States, all of us tagged like so many fish.[6]

With the Clinton administration, Anderson adds, "The smart card idea may have taken an ugly turn." Anderson says he finds alarming the idea by Ira Magaziner, a top Clinton administration planner, that the government's goal is "to create an integrated system with a card that everyone will get at birth." That, Anderson notes, means a "national data bank to store all this information."[7]

The word has been given to the politicians and bureaucrats alike to tout the benefits of mandatory I.D. cards with built-in, tiny computers able to store a thick, extensive dossier on citizens. The truth is far different. With such a system, people can be controlled unlike anything Hitler's Third Reich could possibly imagine.

In 1994, the federal government apparently was on the very precipice of forcing this I.D. Smart Card on us by executive order of the President. Indeed, the U.S. Postal Service (USPS) had been ordered to stand by and prepare to mail out a massive 100 million of the electronic I.D. cards. The card was to be called the *"U.S. Card."*

At a national conference, representatives of the USPS unveiled their prototype U.S. Card. The Postal Service's Chuck Chamberlain carefully explained how the individual's U.S. Card would be interlinked electronically with a multitude of government and private databases. The Department of Health and Human Services, the U.S. Treasury, the I.R.S., the Veteran's Administration, and the full range of police and law enforcement agencies—the ATF, FBI, OSHA, CIA, FDA, EPA, etc.—would have automatic access to the hundreds of pages of private data imbedded in the individual's personal U.S. Card. The agencies and databases would also be able to insert new, updated information on the cards, downloaded from central computers.[8]

Banks would have access to the information, and a central database of digital signatures would be used to validate peoples' authorizations for electronic mail and financial transactions.

After reviewing the Postal Service's glowing, euphoric report on its wonderful, spanking new U.S. Card, one startled authority, dissenting from the common view, observed that:

> In the not-too-distant future, you are likely to find harmless looking Smart Cards in the mail in an official envelope. Without the U.S. Card (or whatever the Smart Card is ultimately called) you won't be able to own property, receive government benefits, get medical attention, conduct bank or credit card transactions, etc. Without it, you can't do anything! Your life will be completely controlled...Executive Orders have already been drafted to adopt the cards and force them on the American people without congressional approval![9]

Clark Matthews, a respected writer in the technological field, concurred with this analysis. In an article entitled, "Danger in the Mail," he wrote:

> Don't look now, but Uncle Sam has some shiny, new shackles with your name on them...There will be one, personalized envelope for every member of your family. You will find a harmless-looking Smart Card contained in each envelope...The government is preparing to reduce every American to total dependence—and near total surveillance through these infamous cards....It is a super Smart Card—a *Tesserea* card, prototyped by the Defense Department and perfected by the distributed-systems experts of the Postal Service, the Treasury

Department, the IRS, and quite possibly the National Security Agency.[10]

Matthews stated his belief that the development of this I.D. card, and the databases which lie at its foundation, would be a monumental leap into a dark, new age of human control and slavery. Referring to the *Card Tech/Security Tech Conference* at which the proposed U.S. Card was introduced to a gullible media and unsuspecting public, Matthews noted that the system is a joint development of both government *and* corporate overlords determined to set up a police state to keep close tabs on a beleaguered citizenry. In other words, the corporate sales managers are more than glad to sell high tech tools to the government which can be used to electronically strangle us! Matthews wryly observed that:

> If Americans are going to be branded or tattooed or implanted with transmitters or otherwise permanently marked and monitored by the government—like slaves in days of old—the folks who attend the (annual) Card Tech/Security Tech Conference generally want to be the ones selling the branding irons.[11]

As Matthews reports, even as they rake in their brisk profits, you can expect the corporate marketing and sales representatives to agree with the politicians. They will assure us that we are to be electronically branded, surveyed, and spied upon "for our own good." The Universal Biometrics I.D. Card, they will tell us in reassuring tones, will be a humanitarian thing—a service item to ease us of so many woes and difficulties. The devil does, indeed, often come disguised as an "angel of light."

The Solution to Our Immigration Problems

For example, the Smart I.D. Card will be portrayed as our salvation and cure for the horrendous plague and

Los Angeles Times

SUNDAY, FEBRUARY 12, 1995
COPYRIGHT 1995 / THE TIMES MIRROR COMPANY / CITY / 478 PAGES

D4　SUNDAY, FEBRUARY 12, 1995 ✱　　　　　　　　　　　　　　　　LOS ANGELES TIMES

Your Money

PERSONAL FINANCE / KATHY M. KRISTOF

On-Line IRS Checks Databases Against Returns

If you have a back tax bill with the Internal Revenue Service, watch out.

In the midst of a program called economic reality, the federal tax agency is going on line, searching for signs of noncompliance as well as electronic records of cars, credit and real estate it can seize from delinquent taxpayers.

The purpose of the new plan is to ferret out tax scofflaws who cheat the federal government out of an estimated $120 billion each year—roughly 17% of total receipts.

A cadre of IRS agents with computers and modems now will be searching records filed with the Department of Motor Vehicles, county tax assessor's offices, credit-reporting companies and the U.S. Bureau of the Census in an effort to find people who are underreporting their business sales, overestimating their deductions or trying to hide assets—or themselves—from federal tax collectors. IRS officials say.

While tax officials have been able to request copies of these records in the past, they generally had to do it by foot—hoofing it down to various county offices and waiting in line to get the data they needed to determine w...

from various [electronic] sources as part of our economic-reality approach," says Frank Keith, an IRS spokesman in Washington. "It is probably the most effective way to uncover unreported income, which is a significant portion of the tax gap."

The new plan, which went into effect late last month, is part of a continuing effort to make tax collection more efficient. In the past

> **'We will be using information from various [electronic] sources as part of our economic-reality approach. It is probably the most effective way to uncover unreported income, which is a significant portion of the tax gap.'**
>
> FRANK KEITH
> IRS spokesman

nationwide find areas where voluntary compliance has gone astray. The IRS will begin compiling a host of demographic information about people in each district. (Districts normally conform to state boundaries, but highly populated states, such as California, have several each.) This information will include currency and banking reports, license information, construction contract information and census data.

For example, the IRS will be looking through census data to determine how many people in a district identified themselves as self-employed and then compare that to the number of tax returns filed with self-employment income, Keith says.

This demographic data has no names attached and will not be used to audit individual returns. Instead it will be used to signal problem areas—such as underreporting of gratuity income or sales figures—and to help districts better focus their audit attention.

The second part of the program is directed at individuals who have delinquent tax bills.

The IRS will get current addresses for taxpayers who have ...ned off the rolls by

taxes—and to help determine whether a taxpayer is lying about income or deductions. The IRS will be suspicious, for example, of a waiter who reports $20,000 in total income but drives a new Porsche.

Property records will be used in the same way, IRS officials note.

The combination of electronic checking on income and electronic checking on deductions and assets should make the IRS far more efficient, tax officials say. However, a few credit experts warn that it also puts a burden on individuals who are under IRS scrutiny.

Why?

The records are not always right. And the tax agency does not need to inform you that it is searching these records, nor is it required to allow you to correct records that are in error. The IRS is not the purveyor of the credit, DMV or property information. Keith explains. Consequently, it cannot correct somebody else's database. Nonetheless, having an IRS agent asking about a long-sold car or assuming there is available credit on what is actually a long-canceled card can be a nightmare for both the taxpayer and the auditor, tax accountants say.

...WHAT DOES THE NEW **SECRET** DATABASE MEAN TO AN ORDINARY TAXPAYER LIKE ME?...

IRS

The Dallas Morning News '95, Universal Press Syndicate 1/22

The IRS, now accessing computer databanks and comparing taxpayers' returns, is becoming more and more tyrannical.

USA TODAY · FRIDAY, AUGUST 5, 1994 · 3A

THE NATION

National ID system stirs fears

Immigration registry proposed

By Maria Puente
USA TODAY

Fear is growing among immigration, privacy and civil-liberties advocates that Americans may soon accept one idea they have resisted for decades: a national identification system.

"It's so disheartening — it's going to be more than an uphill battle," says Janlori Goldman of the Electronic Frontier Foundation, which champions privacy.

The Commission on Immigration Reform, headed by civil rights leader and former Texas congresswoman Barbara Jordan, is calling for a national computer registry containing the names of every citizen or legal alien with a Social Security number or green card.

Employers would check all job applicants against the registry, to prevent illegal immigrants from getting jobs. Jordan says President Clinton should order a pilot program in five states to test the best way to access such a registry.

The plan, which Jordan unveiled this week, calls for a database containing Social Security and Immigration and Naturalization Service records. If set up for California, New York, Texas, Illinois and Florida, the experiment would cover about 94 million people — 36% of the population.

By John Duricka, AP
JORDAN: Wants 5 states to test plan

Pointedly, Jordan cites her civil rights credentials in explaining that the system would not include a national ID card. But many groups insist the plan will inevitably lead to just that.

"A computer registry can't work without a card," says Lucas Guttentag of the American Civil Liberties Union.

Despite the outcry, a broad spectrum of senators and House members have already embraced the idea and introduced bills on it. That suggests the specter of Big Brotherism may be losing its power to frighten Americans and politicians more preoccupied with the real presence of millions of illegal immigrants and the ease with which they use fake documents to get jobs.

"There's very little political momentum to oppose this because it's being done in a back-door way in the name of stemming the tide of illegal immigration," says Goldman.

Opponents are hopeful they can stop the plan by citing the estimated billions of dollars it will cost, the threat to privacy, the potential for discrimination and the inability of the government to maintain accurate records.

"This looks really tempting, but there also have been howls of protest and there may be more hesitation now," says Cecilia Munoz of the National Council of La Raza, a Hispanic civil rights group.

One likely strategy by opponents: Force Congress to vote on the idea. Jordan says the president has authority to unilaterally order a pilot program.

Opponents disagree. "There has to be an up or down vote before taking a step with these far-reaching consequences," says Guttentag.

Jordan's commission is due to issue its first recommendations to Congress on Sept. 30, which might encourage action on a pile of pending bills.

Rep. Xavier Becerra, D-Calif., a leading immigrant defender, says there's strong sentiment to "do something" about illegal aliens. But in an election year "I don't know if I want to put into the hands of Congress ... something as political as immigration," he says.

Other opponents cite more personal arguments. Raul Yzaguirre, president of La Raza, remembers his early years in south Texas when he and other Mexican-Americans carried special cards to prove their citizenship in case they were stopped by the Border Patrol.

"As a 17th-generation Mexican-American, I had to carry a card to prove I was a 'real' American," Yzaguirre says. "No matter what clever names are invented to describe a national identification system, Americans will recognize it for what it is and respond with a resounding 'no.'"

The Orange County Register **WASHINGTON** Wednesday, July 13, 1994

U.S. may issue I.D. cards to citizens

IMMIGRATION: Gov. Pete Wilson wants California to be the test state for 'Employee Verification Registration,' a TV report says.

Reuters

NEW YORK — The federal government, in a response to its inability to control illegal immigration, may soon ask every American to carry a national identity card that would be required when applying for work or social benefits, CBS-TV reported Tuesday.

Called an "Employee Verification Registration," the card would include a photograph, a magnetic strip with vital information, a verified Social Security number and possibly fingerprints, CBS-TV said.

The card could be proposed by the U.S. Commission on Immigration Reform, a bipartisan group that CBS-TV said has already discussed the concept with the White House, which tentatively endorses the idea.

CBS said the card would help the U.S. curb the flow of jobs and public assistance to illegal immigrants who are arriving at U.S. shores in growing numbers seeking work, better shelter and health care.

The care would be required when applying for work or social benefits and would be phased in by age groups over several years, CBS said.

Arizona, California, Florida and Texas, states with large influxes of illegal immigrants, are suing the federal government for reimbursement for immigration-related costs. The states say the money spent to imprison or care for illegals is taking money away from schools, health care and prisons for its citizens.

The states argue that under the Constitution, the U.S. government alone is responsible for regulating immigration. But in failing to do so, the government is responsible for the states' outlays.

California Gov. Pete Wilson said on the newscast that he would ask President Clinton to use his state, which he said has 1.65 million illegal immigrants, to be a test site for the new card.

Wilson could not be reached for comment, but his staff released a letter he sent to Clinton in September calling for Congress to create what he called a "legal-resident eligibility card."

He said California was home to more than half the country's illegal immigrants, creating a great burden on its taxpayers.

"Rather than wait for the development of a nationwide system, I strongly recommend you designate California as the first state in which a working system can be implemented on a fast track," said Wilson's letter.

Kathleen Brown, Wilson's Democratic opponent in the governor's race, could not be reached for comment.

In Santa Ana, Enriqueta Ramos, vice president of Rancho Santiago Community College's board of trustees, said Wilson's support of the Save Our State initiative, which would cut government services for illegal immigrants, and a national identity card could lead California down a dangerous path.

"It will create a neo-Nazi state in the United States where we will be required to tell on each other," she said. "Next thing you know, we'll have tattoos on our bodies."

Lawmakers said the card would be more difficult to counterfeit than other U.S. citizenship documents.

But other lawmakers expressed concern that the program would be ineffective, costly and an incursion into personal privacy.

"Will government really be able to do the job it is claiming? And if not, we've just spent billions of dollars and just given up some major, some severe privacy rights for nothing," Rep. Xavier Becerra, D-Los Angeles, told CBS.

Register staff writer Mary Ann Milbourn contributed to this report.

▶ **POLL:** Should Americans carry a national ID card? **Metro, Page 3**

▶ **POLITICS:** Wilson backs abortion-free GOP platform. **Metro, Page 6**

NATIONAL WEEKLY EDITION

THE WASHINGTON TIMES **COMMENTARY** JUNE 26 - JULY 2 1995 **33**

National I.D. card: Stamp it totalitarian

Few things illustrate the difference between liberals and conservatives as clearly as the different approaches to the immigration issue by liberal Democratic Sen. Dianne Feinstein of California and conservative Republican presidential candidate Pat Buchanan.

Pat Buchanan would act directly against immigrants by a moratorium on even legal immigration and by fortifying the borders. Whatever the merits or demerits of this approach, it focuses its attention directly on immigrants.

Mrs. Feinstein advocates a national identity card that all Americans would be required to have and that all employers would be required to see to prevent hiring illegal aliens. It is the classic liberal response of using a particular problem created by particular people to expand the government's power over other people. The same pattern is seen in liberal responses to crimes committed by people with firearms by cracking down on the far larger number of people with firearms who are committing no crimes.

Nothing polarizes the political left and right like the idea of a national identity card. Yet it is not obvious why, in principle, this should be a liberal-vs.-conservative issue. Everyone should be against people escaping personal responsibility for their

Thomas Sowell

actions by pretending to be somebody else or by relocating to places where their sordid past is not known, thereby permitting them to victimize more innocent people.

Some hard-nosed conservatives have urged that sex offenders in particular be identified and not be allowed to escape their past and continue to prey on unsuspecting neighbors, or those neighbors' children, in the future. Would not a national identity card also permit other kinds of criminals, deadbeat dads and other parasites from escaping their past and jeopardizing other people's futures?

Despite the many potential benefits of a national identity card, the painful fact is that battle lines are drawn over this issue for one reason: We cannot trust the government in general, and liberals in particular, to stop at a national identity card to be used to enforce immigration laws or to deter crime.

Control is the name of the game for liberals, even when they call it "compassion." A national identity card would not only permit even greater government snooping into people's private lives, the information gathered would almost inevitably lead to more laws forcing more people to do more things the way the politicians want them done. It is a down payment on totalitarianism.

Lack of trust is not some purely psychological reaction or a paranoia bred by militias or talk-show hosts. History is full of reasons to distrust governments in general and the political left in particular.

Most Americans probably have no more objection in principle to a national identity card than to some form of gun control. It is only in practice that we know that it will never stop there.

Put differently, many of the benefits that we could get from many policies must be forfeited because of the greater dangers created by the untrustworthiness of those who believe in big government as a means of imposing their own superior wisdom and virtue on others.

At the very moment when the liberal media are blaming "anti-government" feeling for such things as the Oklahoma City bombing and blaming conservative talk-show hosts for promoting such feelings, the Supreme Court of the United States has given a free home demonstration of betrayal of trust by striking down term-limits legislation passed by overwhelming majorities of voters.

Nothing in the Constitution forbids the states to pass such legislation. Moreover, the 10th

> Control is the name of the game for liberals, even when they call it "compassion." A national identity card would almost inevitably lead to more laws forcing more people to do more things the way the politicians want them done. It is a down payment on totalitarianism.

Amendment clearly sets forth the principle that the federal government can do only what it is specifically authorized to do, while the states and the people can do whatever they are not forbidden to do. But the learned justices decided to turn this principle upside down — perhaps they should call it the 01 Amendment now — and claim that the states need specific authorization to act.

All this dishonesty served only to impose their preferences and prejudices on the rest of us. Instead of saying where in the Constitution such laws as term limits are forbidden, the Supreme Court majority quoted previous decisions by their predecessors, who also made it up as they went along.

So long as what the justices made up was what the liberal media liked, they went along too. Those justices who think that the Constitution means what it says — Justices Clarence Thomas and Antonin Scalia being the most prominent of these on the present court — are treated as fuddy-duddies and party-poopers.

Betrayals of trust from the bench, from the Congress and from presidents are what has spread such profound distrust. If ever we are to gain the benefits that would be possible in a society where we could trust one another more, that will have to come from "responsible" government officials showing that they are worthy of more trust. It will not come from scapegoating talk-show hosts.

Thomas Sowell, an economist and a senior fellow at the Hoover Institution, is a nationally syndicated columnist.

The American people fear a national I.D. card, but the politicians are determined to cram it down our throats.

flood of illegal immigrants violating U.S.A. borders. The truth is that our politicians care little that we are besieged by illegal aliens. Most U.S. senators and congressmen and state governors are rabid supporters of multiculturalism. They viciously attack anyone who opposes foreign influx as an "ethnocentric, narrow-minded, antiquated relic of bigotry." When the liberals like California Senator Diane Feinstein and Massachusetts Senator Edward Kennedy begin to promote a national I.D. card to stem the tide of illegal immigration, you know the fix is in. These politicians *love* illegal immigration, make no mistake about it—it feathers their political nest.

What they also love is *control*, and under the guise of controlling immigration, they know they will be controlling *us*, the bonafide citizenry, *not* the waves of foreigners preparing to crash our borders.

That is why we must be wide awake when we are propagandized by the media with reports that high tech holds the answer to the illegal immigration crisis.

R. E. McMaster, in his insightful *The Reaper* newsletter, keenly analyzed a news item from *USA Today* on a gigantic, new government computer project by reporting:

> The U.S. Immigration and Naturalization Service announced Tuesday a $300 million computer software contract, which could take the U.S. closer to an era of Big Brother—a national ID card. The INS claimed the contract as its biggest ever and touts it as a model of the Clinton administration's effort to "reinvent government" and as a way to reduce paperwork. The computer system will take three years to be operational. The U.S. Commission on Immigration Reform will issue its first report on September 30 and is expected to recommend creation of a national database to prevent illegal immigrants from getting jobs...It's national I.D. time with all the loss of freedom it represents.[12]

My insider sources in Washington, D.C., have told me of their belief that the $300 million contract for Big

Brother's computer networking software reported in *USA Today* is part and parcel of the comprehensive, Beast 666 *Project L.U.C.I.D.* net. Their report is confirmed by an announcement from an international magazine in 1996 concerning a proposal—by two powerful U.S. legislators—for the creation of a behemoth, six billion dollar computer I.D. system.[13] The expensive system would, supposedly, better control illegal immigration. The two legislators claim that only with such a gargantuan system as this could the United States put a lid on the illegal overflow of immigrants.

Under the proposed system, Americans would have to pay $70 for a "worker's card," a Smart I.D. Card which they would be required to carry on their persons at all times under threat of arrest, imprisonment, and fines. Workers' I.D. cards would be integrated into an international employee identification registry, or database.[14]

I believe that the mind-warping, intrusive, *six billion dollar* computer I.D. system called for by Wyoming Senator Alan Simpson and Texas Representative Lamar Smith is, in fact, *Project L.U.C.I.D.*, complete with its police state ability to track, trace, and enslave all of the earth's nearly six billion inhabitants!

The New Gestapo State Emerges

Would they really arrest you if you failed to apply for and keep their Smart I.D. Card on your possession at all times? What will happen to resisters who have no cards in their wallet, purse, or pocket? Gary Pelphrey, of Georgia, writing in the *Marietta Daily Journal*, recently gave us a foretaste of the spellbinding days soon to come with a shocking, eyewitness account. Pelphrey says that the current crackdown is on aliens, but "who will be rounded up next?"

> When you get to be 60 years old, it seems to me that you ought to pretty much be out of possibilities for things to

just shock the bejeebies out of you. I really expected that by now I would have developed what some might call a fine patina to protect myself against the onslaught of ridiculous sights and sounds.

Not so. This morning a fellow lawyer in our building came running from down the hall yelling, "You ought to see what's happening across the street at the new courthouse under construction."

I followed him to a corner window. What we saw is something I had theretofore only seen on TV, and then only in foreign dictatorships.

Overhead, a helicopter circled, at about I would guess 100 to 150 feet, well below any authorized FAA minimums for an area as congested as downtown Marietta.

The street between the Cobb County Courthouse and the new building under construction was sealed off by 8 to 12 cars with licenses ranging from Rockdale County to Dade County, Florida. One was driven by a particularly snippy female agent wearing a black uniform and had no license plate at all. There was also a bus to transport the "guilty" off to somewhere.

My call to the Marietta 911 dispatcher yielded the news that the local police didn't know anything at all about what was happening about a block away from their headquarters.

The agents all said they were too busy to explain what they were doing, and under what authority.

In point of fact, what they appeared to be doing was rounding up every one at this particular work site who had a Hispanic appearance, and, if he could not prove himself a citizen, trussing his hand behind him with

some plastic contraptions like we use at home to close a
smelly garbage bag.

The four to six people trussed up like this (no one
seemed to know how many) were whisked away,
presumably either in the helicopter or one of the fleet of
sedans, or maybe even the bus, to places we can only
guess about. Do we have gulags?

The time has come for us to realize that if the
government wants to flex its enormous muscles, it will.
And as long as we, the unaffected, stand idly by
watching, it can. It's time, too, for us to realize that there
are no unaffected.

Those in authority in our government are not going to
start out by rounding up the Girl Scouts or the Rotary
Club. They're going to start with some outcast group,
some politically-bankrupt section of our society, like, say,
an off-the-wall religious cult or maybe an easy-to-isolate-
by-looks minority such as Hispanics. But that religious
group did, in fact, have rights, and probably one of them
was that their children could not be barbecued by federal
agents.

These Hispanic-looking folks have rights, too. If they are
citizens, they don't have to carry around identification
papers any more than we do. I have on my person right
now proof that I can drive a car, that I can gain entry
into the Cobb County Courthouse and can buy food at a
discount at Cub Foods. But with what's on my person
right now, I can't prove I'm a citizen. Can you?

Now I find myself re-living the incident this morning
and talking to others who were there. Each of us stood
in awe, and, when we were really ready to admit it,
frightened at being this close to such a raw use (or
abuse) of overwhelming governmental power. (What)
kept coming to mind were the brown-shirts of World

War II, the black-shirted Nazis, the jackbooted thugs that spirited Anne Frank away.[15]

Unfortunately, a dumbed-down, mass citizenry constantly fed New World Order propaganda by the media and being turned into unthinking, nihilistic "space cadets" and ruffians by the public education system, cannot fathom what lies just ahead in our radiant, high tech future nightmare. I thank God, however, for those Americans and foreign citizens who *do* understand the deep prophetic significance of what is transpiring. Here, for instance, is what one of my correspondents, Mr. Steven Heinecke, of Columbia Heights, Minnesota, recently wrote to me:

> In my estimation, this nation and the world itself is poised at a critical intersection, and the coming months will determine the very nature of humanity's future...Once this national I.D. card comes on line, and the money, fuel, and food crisis get a push, there will be a severe outbreak of civil strife and crime, poverty, and violence of unprecedented proportions in the land, giving government the perfect excuse to clamp down on American citizens and disarm us all.

Mr. Heinecke also stated: "Friends within the postal service tell me that management is working hard and fast to equip every post office in the nation with countertop scanners...I have to wonder if these scanners will be used for the new I.D. cards, under the pretext that the new, computerized system will prevent terrorists from sending mail bombs."

My friend and correspondent is right. Every day, the press is pushing computer databank registries and Smart I.D. Cards as the solution to illegal immigration, gun control, teenage violence, hate crimes, terrorism, and other ills. In a recent, Associated Press story from Harrisburg, Pennsylvania, we were told of how electronic fingerprinting and a national database could prevent welfare fraud. Representative Tom Petrone, of Allegheny, Pennsylvania, contended: "The state should join a national fingerprint (biometrics) database that would prevent people from using phony names to fraudulently obtain welfare cash grants and food stamps."[16]

In California, to prevent fake drivers licenses being passed off, the state recently implemented a color photo process for licenses, with magnetic strips, see-through hologram imprints, and other special features.

Obviously, this is a precursor to the state's inclusion of its drivers license program in the international *L.U.C.I.D.* net system. Many other states are also implementing new drivers license I.D. procedures.

California's State Department of Motor Vehicles, in its Drivers License Information Memo 91-1, states:

> The new process involves capturing and storing the applicant's photo, fingerprint, and signature in digitized form...The (state) will create a centralized data base which can be accessed by Headquarters Information Services Unit later to retrieve, display, or print documents.

News reports indicate that, like California, practically all of the 50 states are in the process of installing new systems for drivers licenses, often incorporating biometric measurements such as digitization of iris scan, fingerprint, photograph, bar code, social security number, traffic and criminal history, etc. This, plus the fact that steps are being taken to link and network computers for the 50 states, gives us an indication of the powerful grip our hidden controllers have on this nation.[17]

Still, the maximum control can be obtained through issuance of a *centralized*—that is, a national, Smart I.D. Card. *Project L.U.C.I.D.* will go even further, implementing a *global* system of I.D. cards. These will be Smart Cards, linked by satellite and by fiber optic lines with all law enforcement, government, and corporate computer networks around the world. This will fulfill the prophecy in Revelation 13 that all the world shall worship the beast and take his mark, name, or number of his name.

Healthcare Plan a Conspiratorial Fraud?

Since total and absolute control can be obtained only by a police state bureaucracy, efforts have escalated in recent years to require a national I.D. card. Upon Bill Clinton's election as President, Secretary of Health and Human Services Donna Shalala and Massachusetts Senator Edward Kennedy jointly developed a $100 million plan to require all children and babies to have a dossier established in a national computer registry to insure "universal mandatory vaccinations."[18]

When patriotic Americans rose up to protest, the U.S. Senate quietly shelved the deceptive Shalala-Kennedy proposal.

The Clinton administration next surfaced with its mandatory healthcare plan. A key component of this plot to socialize medical care was the requirement of a computer I.D. card for every American, linked in to a master computer control network. Martin Anderson, writing in *The Washington Times,* cautioned about the hidden agenda and the potential horrors of Clinton's massive, taxpayer-supported, healthcare extravaganza:

> There is something in the plan that may be far worse than the new taxes that will be heaped upon us, or the increased physical pain and suffering we will endure as the result of endless waiting lines for health care. That something is a device that will invade our personal privacy as it has never been invaded before.

> President Clinton held it in his hand when he addressed the nation, proudly waving it like a small American flag. Only it wasn't a flag; it was the "health security card"— his slick name for a national identity card. Under his plan a new National Health Board would establish "national, unique identifier numbers" for every single one of us.

> Every time we visit a doctor or get a prescription or go

to the hospital the records would be "captured, retained and transmitted" via the identity card. Those records would feed into "electronic networks," and the federal government would set up "national standards for electronic data transmission."

That's right folks. A national computer databank, holding all our most personal medical records, would be open to the curious, prying eyes of government bureaucrats, other "authorized" people and, of course, any unauthorized snoopers who figure out how to crack the system.

What makes this privacy nightmare possible are striking advances in technology. That pretty, red, white and blue card the president was waving around is called a "smart card." Some cards contain computer chips, some have optical storage devices. That kind of card is now, today, capable of holding thousands of pages of personal data, computerized fingerprints, a mug shot and even your voice.

Once in place, the card will be impossible to get rid of. The pressures to expand the uses of such a technological tattoo will be strong and inexorable. If everyone must have one, why not add our Social Security numbers to it, enabling government officials to correlate our health records with other personal records?

The government could require all who apply for welfare to produce the card to prevent fraud. We could catch illegal aliens with a "no card, no work" law. The police could use it to maintain a permanent record of all our parking tickets and speeding violations, checking the entire record every time a motorist is stopped. We could require all gun buyers to record the registration number of the gun on the card...

If President Clinton's so-called health security card becomes a reality, we can kiss goodbye to privacy as we now know it. Of course, on the bright side, one can think of the card as an intimate, constant reminder of President Bill and Hillary, and all they are doing for us.[19]

Antony Sutton whose books, such as *The Secret Establishment*, are mother lodes of information about the global elite and their quest to enslave us, also issued a Red Alert concerning the Clinton administration's concealed agenda in the health card affair. It is not our health care in which the elite are interested, he wrote. It is the tracking and control of we, the people. Moreover, Sutton says he finds little difference between the "internal passport" once required by the U.S.S.R. of its citizens and the proposed, new Smart I.D. Card to be imposed by the United States:

> For months we have been puzzled by Clinton's insistence on UNIVERSAL health care, that *everyone* must be covered by his bureaucratic, top-heavy program. Then we received samples of the health benefits card that Clinton proposes to distribute universally. It is an extraordinary device—*much more than an ID card.*
>
> The card is about the size and shape of a credit card but is actually a data storage card (up to *2000 pages* of information) using the latest optical recording technology. The card can record anything, *i.e. data, graphics, pictures, voice prints, fingerprints.* It can be transmitted via any form of telecommunications or used off-line, (i.e., a stand alone optical card reader.) It is non-erasable, impervious to magnetic and electrostatic fields and withstands temperatures up to 200° F. *It is the ideal Big Brother tracking device.*
>
> In case you need to know, it is manufactured by Drexler Technology Corporation, Mountain View, California (telephone for the Laser Card Systems Corporation is (415) 969-4428, fax (415) 967-6524).
>
> Now you know *why* Mr. Clinton wants a UNIVERSAL

health care system. Nothing to do with health, but *a lot to do with getting us all catalogued on Big Brother computers.*

The U.S. Postal Service is all geared up to send out 100 million such cards within a few months and Drexler capacity is 100 million a year minimum.

The computer press even tracked down *already signed Executive Orders to force* the cards into use. *PC Week* asked the White House for comment and received a brush off "no comment."

The next stage will be the ID biochip insert placed under the skin at birth.

Elsewhere, we comment that Mrs. Clinton is disturbed at public reaction to administration proposals. *What does she expect?* Is there any difference between the Clinton Universal ID Card and the Soviet internal passport? Except that Clinton's is more efficient!

Final note: Why does the administration want *voice print* recognition capability on a *health card? The latest surveillance techniques use a super computer hookup to recognize voice prints,* and you can be instantly identified anywhere you accept a phone call.[20]

Invasive Powers of a Malignant Nature

If anyone doubts that the plan to require all citizens to carry a national I.D. card and to establish a government-run central database with invasive powers is malignant, I offer the sage comments of Thomas J. DiLorenzo, professor of economics at Loyola College in Baltimore and adjunct scholar at the Cato Institute. In an editorial in *The Wall Street Journal,* Dr. DiLorenzo compared the Clinton plan for the United States to the national socialist healthcare system implemented by Italy's Fascist dictator, Benito

Mussolini, in the 1930s. DiLorenzo finds striking similarities between the two.[21]

Apparently, the 1990s plan for America's socialized healthcare and a police state I.D. card is simply a warmed over, more high tech version of what the poor citizenry of Italy were once forced to endure. Dr. DiLorenzo concludes that:

> Most people equate fascism only with its racism and anti-Semitism, but there was also an economic philosophy, known as "corporatism" that was part of its ideology. The Clintons have adopted 1930s-era corporatism as the organizing principle of their health reform.

> Contrary to the hoary slogans about Mussolini "making the trains run on time," the truth is that corporatism was an unmitigated economic disaster for the Italian people. Let's hope that this failure will not be repeated in the U.S.[22]

Fortunately, President Bill Clinton's healthcare scam never made it into law. Again, an informed citizenry rose to the occasion and demanded that Congress *not* vote their approval. Sadly, few of the complainers were upset about the potential for abuse by Big Brother's Smart I.D. Card. Most simply felt the multi-billion dollar price tag to socialize medical services was too excessive.

But, believe me, the conspirators are not finished with us yet. My sources tell me that they are *determined* that the people of the United States will have a Fascist-controlled healthcare system, with computerized, government-run databanks and an I.D. card. So look for this proposal to be resurrected soon—certainly by the year 2000.

"It's For Your Own Good," They Say

The establishment's most recent "excuse" for requiring the I.D. card is the immigration "crisis." We are being

FLASHPOINT

A NEWSLETTER MINISTRY OF TEXE MARRS

"The Truth Shall Make You Free"
John 8:32

LIVING TRUTH MINISTRIES   OCTOBER 1994

The New MARC Card—"Don't Leave Home Without It!"

"*National Citizen I.D. is Proposed*" read the headline in *USA Today* (July 13, 1994). Reporting from Washington, D.C., news reporter Maria Puente informed readers that, "All U.S. citizens and legal immigrants would receive the equivalent of a national I.D. card under an expected proposal to Congress by the Commission on Immigration Reform, chaired by former Democrat Congresswoman Barbara Jordan."

This announcement of a pending national I.D. card raised hackles among patriotic Americans. A veritable firestorm of protest flooded congressional phone and fax lines. Stunned by the negative response, the Jordan Commission backtracked, announcing that the I.D. card will be delayed *for now*. Instead, the Commission proposes that "*a national data base*" be established. In effect, this would be a Big Brother/Big Sister computer system with every citizen's primary data entered therein.

The Master Plan

But, watch out! The federals have not given up on their idea of a national I.D. card. They need this to control the citizen peons. Their master plan calls, first, for a photo, bar coded, I.D. card of every man, woman, and child, complete with a built-in computer chip dossier and file. The I.D. cards of so-called "Enemies of the State" (yes, friends, you and me!) will be so designated.

However, once the populace gets used to their spiffy new I.D. cards and sees how simple it is to buy, sell, and apply for a job or a loan with it, the federals will advance to Step 2 of "The Plan."

Under Step 2, the government will inform the duped masses that the Smart I.D. Card is no longer useful. In fact, the bureaucrats will lament, the card is an onerous burden. It takes up room in one's wallet or a purse. It can be lost or stolen. Wouldn't it be easier and more convenient and efficient for us to just insert a tiny microchip in the forehead or right hand of everyone? Then you really cannot "leave home without it!"

Mexico's I.D. Card—A CIA Project?

The government, therefore, will first try to convince us that we *need* the national I.D. card. To accomplish this propaganda feat, several experimental tests are underway. Down in Mexico during the recent national elections, the American CIA and their Mexican NAFTA partners issued citizens the new, computerized "Voter's I.D. Card." Developed jointly by U.S. multinational

Texe Marrs

corporations IBM, Booz-Allen and Hamilton, Oracle (a California software company), and Polaroid, the corrupt Mexican government spent $730 million to deliver the cards to that nation's 46 million voters. The money most probably came from a secret, CIA "spook" banking account.

Now, if you believe that this I.D. card, Mexico's first national identification system, will ever guarantee honest, free elections down Mexico way, I have this great bridge, located in the midst of Louisiana's most scenic swamplands, that I'd like to sell you at a bargain price.

I.D. Cards: A Worldwide Project of the Illuminati

The Illuminati who now control Washington D.C. have given top priority to the issuance of microchip I.D. cards to every man, woman, and child on planet Earth. Already, in the Netherlands, a new law now requires citizens to carry I.D. cards on their person. The card contains the individual's tax-file number, name, address, nationality, etc. Persons not able to produce the card upon demand of police are being arrested and jailed (*Source: Ministry for Justice, The Hague, The Netherlands*).

In Britain, Prime Minister John Major recently asked Parliament to decree that such a card be required of all citizens (*The Sunday Times, March 27, 1994*). The I.D. cards are to be issued by British authorities until January 1, 1995 when the new, European Economic Community cards will be available for all citizens of Europe.

Meanwhile, in Australia, I.D. cards will also be mandatory beginning in 1995 (*The Sydney Morning Herald, June 11, 1994*).

And Now, the MARC Card

While the CIA and the Mexicans are using the citizenry down South for experimental purposes and the Illuminati in Europe and Australia are plotting their own strategies for forcing I.D. cards on the people, here in the good old U.S.A. the government department that Bill Clinton truly loathes—the Department of Defense—is assisting the Clinton administration in conducting yet another Big Brother/Big Sister test. This

MARC

ROBERT L. WALLINGFORD, JR.
20/123456789   TAMC
RANK   SERVICE   STATUS   DATE OF BIRTH   BLOOD TYPE
MGYSGTUSMC   AD   19610930   O-POS

In my Flashpoint newsletter of October 1994, I exposed the DOD plan to require all U.S. Armed Forces personnel to carry the "MARC" Card. (Note: For a free subscription to Flashpoint, phone toll free 1-800-234-9673, or write to Living Truth Publishers, 1708 Patterson Road, Austin, Texas 78733.

told that, for just a pittance (eight billion dollars to start!), we can solve the illegal alien problem by implementing the national I.D. card system and setting up a comprehensive, citizen database registry. To sweeten their offer, the elite are telling the citizenry that the I.D. card system will *save* taxpayers billions of dollars spent today on healthcare and welfare for aliens inside the U.S.A. Also, we are assured that the I.D. card will mean more jobs for bonafide American citizens.

While these are legitimate concerns, it would be shameful for the American people to trade in their constitutional right to privacy and give up a patriotic heritage of over 200 years for the economic advantages that are *claimed* to accrue from a Beast 666 Smart I.D. Card network.

In fact, it is doubtful that economic advantage can be gained from the elite's high tech control system. Most likely, jobs and factories will continue to flow overseas, because the corporate Fascists who now rule America find it loathsome and disgusting to pay American workers decent wages when they can hire slave labor in Red China and Russia for 10 to 25 cents per hour!

We've seen that the federal government has adeptly used excuse after excuse to cram a national I.D. card system down our collective throats. The latest proposal is to mandate I.D. cards for all school children under the *Goals 2000* national education program. Another plan, by the U.S. Labor Department, will require I.D. cards for all workers, to be connected electronically with a *National Job Training and Employment* computer database. Secretary Robert Reich, at a press conference, told enthused media representatives how this idea will result in "better job relocation opportunities" for Americans out of work.

Maybe Mr. Reich was referring to the job openings soon to come available for security guards, facilities keepers, kitchen personnel, etc., at detention centers and concentration camps reportedly now being readied for government dissenters, patriotic constitutionalists, biblical Christians, and other victims.

Government Action and Public Reaction

A clue to the government's future intentions and also to how some people may react perhaps can be found in what is happening at U.S. military installations. There, our soldiers, marines, airmen, and sailors are being forced *against their will* to accept the government's, high tech I.D. card, ominously and prophetically called the *"MARC Card."* On April 1995, at the Card Tech/Security Tech Conference in Washington, D.C., Gemplus Card International Corp. announced that the Department of Defense (DOD) had placed a huge order for the corporation to initially supply 60,000 of the microprocessors used in the military's new I.D. card. Since then, the company has continued to supply the microprocessors.[23]

Gemplus is also providing the *Gemplus Docket Reader*, linked up to central computers, to enable the DOD to "read" the identity cards at sites throughout the world. The Gemplus corporation is a giant firm with sales offices worldwide and manufacturing facilities in France and Germany. The corporation, in a press release dated July 1995, boasted it could produce *20 million* of their Smart Cards per month. In 1994, the company shipped *140 million* cards.

Evidently, not all of our nation's proud military men and women are happy about being forced to forego their hard-earned privacy and submit to the MARC card. Realizing the dread, prophetic meaning and implications, some brave servicemen are stubbornly refusing the card. Punishment and retribution has been swift and certain. So far, three men in uniform have been courtmartialed. U.S. Air Force Technical Sergeant Warren Sinclair of Hampton, Virginia, was one of these punished by courtmartial. Sergeant Sinclair disobeyed an order to provide blood and saliva samples for the required DNA registry.[24]

Christianity Today magazine recently carried a story about a marine who also is considering disobeying orders to submit to the MARC Card. In an article entitled, "Marine

Worries I.D. is Satanic," *Christianity Today's* Jennifer Ferranti reported:

> A 26-year-old marine pilot who is a Christian sees an eerie resemblance between a multitechnology automated reader card (MARC) that marines are required to wear at his base in Kaneohe Bay, Hawaii, and another mark—the mark of the beast described in the Book of Revelation.
>
> Capt. Joel Kirk has thus far avoided having his picture taken for the new identification card, which carries name, rank, serial number—and a two-megabyte computer chip designed to hold whatever information and records the military deems appropriate.
>
> The military says it will use the MARC to deploy troops faster. But Kirk worries it will be required for every kind of transaction. "When you take that card and they put the reader scanners into the commissaries and exchanges and weapons draw, you become a slave to that system," he says. And there's little difference, Kirk suggests, between a mark *held* in your hand and one *implanted* in your hand.[25]

Saints and Heroes Pay the Price

Marine Corps Captain Joel Kirk has obviously read the Bible. He knows that the MARC Card will make slaves of men and women. It seems that our captive servicemen are becoming the first victims of the Beast 666 Universal Human Control System. Good people like Sergeant Sinclair and Captain Kirk are practicing a "just say no policy"—and they're paying the price for their righteous refusal to serve Baal. They are genuine, end-times heroes. Now comes the poignant question: What will you do when, someday soon, they demand that *you* accept the 666 Smart Card that shall be your personal passport to international oppression and ruthless control?

And such as do wickedly against the covenant shall he *(the Antichrist and beast)* corrupt by flatteries: but the people that do know their God shall be strong, and do exploits. (Daniel 11:32)

And they that understand among the people shall instruct many: yet they shall fall by the sword, and by flame, by captivity, and by spoil many days. (Daniel 11:33)

Many shall be purified, and made white, and tried; but the wicked shall do wickedly: and none of the wicked shall understand; but the wise shall understand. (Daniel 12:10)

FOUR

Implantable Biochips:
A "Do or Die" Situation

S oon, we'll all have a biochip injected under our skin, and when we go into stores we'll do our buying and selling with it by scanning our hands across modified store scanners which will automatically debit our bank accounts." This is the prediction of my good friend, Terry Cook, one of the top authorities in the field of implantable biochips. For years, Terry has been steadily warning people of the dangers inherent in this fantastic, new technological tool of control.

My own pioneering work in this field dates from the mid-1970s, when I first began my in-depth research into the complex, and fascinating, subject of mind control through implanted, computer devices in human beings. My early studies were in the area of robots, and resulted in five books on robotics and artificial intelligence. Some of these books were published by top, New York publishing houses and were chosen as main selections by the Computer Book Club, the Electronic Book Club, and the World Future Society.

In 1987, *Mega Forces*, my first book exploring the prophetic dimensions of what I call "black science" or "dark technology" was published by Tyndale House Publishers, later to be reprinted by Living Truth Publishers. On pages 27 and 28 of *Mega Forces*, I stated:

> Experts in robotics and artificial intelligence are working hard to perfect lifelike robots with silicon chip brains

that can think, make independent judgments, and take actions *without* the assistance of humans. By the year 2000 or shortly thereafter, biological engineering—which has already created bacterial life-forms in the lab—will wed its knowledge to that of the roboticists. "Biological chips"—fleshly substances—will be used to construct the brains of robots.

Several companies are already working on this project...This will be made possible by new achievements in robotics technology looming on the horizon, achievements which include the use of materials similar to human flesh and the manufacture of organic "brains," or biological computer units. This is not science fiction malarkey. It is reality.

Gorham International, a highly regarded technology research and development firm in Gorham, Maine, says that a billion dollar biochip industry is rapidly developing. According to the firm, the biochip will be a stupendous technological advance drawing on "quantum engineering" that will eventually produce the ultimate molecular computer. "The biochip revolution has indeed begun. Scores of technologists in public and private laboratories around the world are joining in a research effort that will occupy the talents of tens of thousands in the 1990s."[1]

Stunning Disclosures

Notice that my book, *Mega Forces*, first became available to the general public in 1987. At the time, my disclosures about the coming, new, implantable biochips which would revolutionize human—and robotic—life as we know it stunned many readers. They simply couldn't believe that the science was that far advanced. But it was. Even as I wrote *Mega Forces*, I was becoming aware of super-secret experiments by government and corporate laboratories in which human subjects—usually unwilling and unsuspecting guinea pigs—were having computer chips and transmitting devices implanted into their cerebral hemispheres (e.g. their brains), auditory (ear) organs, and elsewhere in their bodies.

Of course, all of this highly classified and hush-hush research was supposedly being done "for the advancement of science, for the good of all mankind." *Sure* it was!

In reality, from the vantage point of the elite, there are only two reasons to develop and implement a universal system in which every man, woman, and child will be injected with a computer biochip. One, of course, is the factor of money. There is big money ahead for the high tech corporations who receive government contracts to implant biochips in up to six billion human beings. But the primary reason for this system's use is *control*. The implantable biochip provides incredible potential for the Illuminati and their stooges to gain absolute, permanent control over the minds of men.

As I wrote in *Mega Forces*, "Never in human history have tyrants and madmen had such tools—tools which they can use to plunder minds and terrorize an entire population...One shudders to think of the power this capability might give corrupt leaders or thugs bent on controlling the mind-thoughts of individuals."[2]

This is precisely the grim message I have been propounding for over a decade now. Finally, a few other thoughtful people are starting to take note.

Recently, I was quoted at length in *The Boulder Weekly*, a Colorado newspaper, which carried a cautionary article highlighting the downside of biochip implants. Later, *Media Bypass* magazine published this excerpt:

> *The Boulder Weekly* quoted Texe Marrs, a political science professor and author of *"Dark Secrets of the New Age,"* as saying the implants will likely "be used by a One World government to track people and exercise control over their lives...There is a lot of evidence that chips are under development that can tie into the brain's neuro-network, giving someone who controls the chip the

ability to control the thoughts and actions of anyone who contains the chip."[3]

I'm sure that many who read that edition of *The Boulder Weekly* must have scoffed and sneered. But the skeptics and cynics are, regrettably, *abominably ignorant*. They are oblivious to the dangers of what Stanley Wellborn, in *U.S. News and World Report*, called the "biochip revolution" and the "race to create a living computer."[4]

Eavesdropping on the Brain

Only a few of the authorities in the field of biochips and implantable devices are joining me in running up the red flag about the mind control abuse potential of this technology. Most see implantable biochips as offering a marvelous and bright future for mankind. One such expert is G. Harry Stine. In his book, *The Silicon Gods*, Stine foresaw a near future in which men could become like gods through the use of "intelligence amplifiers" implanted in the brains.[5]

Stine wrote that, very soon, intelligence amplifiers— tiny microchip devices either implanted in humans or capable of being temporarily connected to the human brain and sensory channels—will actually allow others to "get inside a person's head." With such devices, we will possess the astonishing ability to hear the thoughts of others.[6]

Researchers have made rapid progress to bring this to reality. An eye-opening article in *Science News* reported that, "New electronic techniques are being developed to eavesdrop on the brain."

According to *Science News*, "The techniques, under study at the University of Michigan at Ann Arbor, in AT&T labs, and elsewhere, will allow outsiders to direct a person's brain cell conversations and talk directly to the individual's brain neurons. The article also said that current research centers on the eventual employment of integrated circuit chips that can be either implanted in the brain or overlaid with brain cells."[7]

Will the *L.U.C.I.D.* net someday integrate this brain control technology into its global system? Even Stine, an optimist who believes that man will not allow the abuse of these capabilities, nevertheless warns:

> It also contains the seeds of unimaginable evil: the actual control of human minds by other humans. Not brainwashing. Not propaganda. Not any of the ancient and well-proven means of mentally or physically imposing one person's will by police action or torture. But the actual control of the human mind.[8]

An Army of Zombies

Isolated news reports about government research into biochips bring evidence of a frightening future for mankind once the implanting of these devilish devices is initiated on a mass scale. In 1995, Pat Cooper, a reporter for *Defense News*, wrote an article entitled, "Naval Research Lab Attempts to Meld Neurons and Chips." Cooper quoted Lawrence Korb, a former top DOD official, as saying that, "The studies by the Defense Department produce an army of zombies."[9]

The research, Cooper noted, "has captured the interest of the U.S. intelligence community."[10] After observing that there are unlimited useful applications of the rising, new technology, Cooper quoted Steve Aftergood, a senior analyst for the Washington-based Federation of American Scientist, who stated, "For all the desirable applications, it (smart biochips) may have horrific applications."[11]

Speaking before the Defense Electronics Symposium, sponsored by the American Defense Preparedness Association, in Arlington, Virginia, in 1995, William Tolles, former associate director of research of the Naval Research Laboratory, stated: "Once this technology is proved, you could *control* a living species."[12]

Kyle Olson, of the Chemical and Biological Arms Control Institute, concurs with this alarming analysis. "The door swings in two directions," said Olson. "You've got this Frankenstein-type weapon on one hand, and it can deal with problems of the human condition on the other."[13]

On the positive side, Olson suggested, you could, for example, program memory into an implantable biochip, "pop it into your head and instantly know French or another language."[14]

The overly cheery perspective that man will use the new biochip technology only for good seems to be a unique facet of today's optimistic, high technology society and mind-set. Thus, reporter Teresa Allen, in a news feature entitled, "Future Shocker: Biochip—Science Fiction Technology Here," dramatically writes:

Don't reach for your wallet at the check-out counter.

After your food items have been priced, tallied and bagged, simply pass your hand over the computer code scanner used on the groceries, and the bill will be automatically deducted from your checking account.

Or consider this: A powerful "biochip" made from living protein that, once surgically implanted in the brain, could make it possible to program or "upload" an unlimited amount of information into the mind—without having ever cracked open a book.

Impossible? The plot of a science fiction novel?

The technology to accomplish such fantastic feats is already here or, as in the case of the living biochip, in the process of being developed, says Tim Willard, executive officer of the World Future Society, a Washington D.C.-based organization that claims 27,000 members worldwide, including "Future Shock" author Alvin Toffler.

"But just suggest something like an implant in humans and the social outcry is tremendous," Willard said.

"While people over the years may have grown accustomed to artificial body parts, there is definitely a strong aversion to things being implanted. It's the 'Big Brother is watching' concept. People would be afraid that all of their thoughts and movements were being monitored. It wouldn't matter if the technology was there or not. People would still worry."[15]

But obviously, Tim Willard isn't worried. Nor, I believe, are the majority of Americans. Millions of citizens, intoxicated by today's modern, high tech wizardry, are oblivious to the ominous dangers that this technology will be abused. Unlike Christians who know their Bible, men such as Tim Willard and other influential members of the pro-globalist, New Age-oriented World Future Society, appear overly confident in man's ability to control government.

Reporting that within 15 to 20 years, "the regular microchip will be outclassed and replaced by a biochip made out of living protein," Willard said that the technology behind the biochip is "fairly uncomplicated and, with a little refinement, could be used in a variety of human applications." [16]

"Conceivably, a number could be assigned at birth and go with a person throughout life," Willard said.[17]

Most likely, he added, it would be implanted on the back of the right or left hand for convenience, "so that it would be easy to scan."[18]

"It could be used as a universal identification card that would replace credit cards, passports, that sort of thing," Willard said. "At the checkout stand at a supermarket, you would simply pass your hand over a scanner and your bank account would automatically be debited."[19]

Bible Prophecy Fulfilled

How fascinating it is for us to realize that Willard's visionary, future use of the implantable biochip would perfectly fulfill Bible prophecy. For example, Revelation

13 warns of the Mark of the Beast to be given, either in the forehead or in the right hand. Also, the use of the biochip for commercial purchases brings to mind the prophecy that, in the last days, no man may buy or sell, save he that had the mark, or the name, or the number of the beast.

What Mr. Willard sees as a positive and beneficial reality for man's immediate future will, in fact, usher in the nightmarish era of control, tribulation, and persecution foreseen by God's prophets some 1900 years ago!

There seems to be no end of the "Frankenstein-type" uses to which the biochip can be applied. For example, what of an implantable biochip developed by Antichrist scientists which is programmed to cause humans to love Satan and hate Jesus Christ? Could not such a biochip, popped into or injected into their brain, instantly produce servile multitudes of people eager and willing to worship the image of the Beast and do his bidding, even to the extent of going out and killing all born again Christians?

This is not absurd reasoning. It is not science fiction. We are discussing realistic technology, available *now*, which will be applied in the near future exactly as written in Bible prophecy. Glenn Krawczyk, for example, in an article in *Nexus* magazine entitled, "Mind Control and The New World Order," provides documented evidence of mind control, biomedical devices implanted in human beings. He also presents a detailed bibliography of source references.[20]

If the concept of a biochip-controlled army of future zombies bent on destroying resisters to an Antichrist New World Order seems far-fetched, certainly the proposals now being seriously considered for implementation by government and corporate officials should awaken at least some Americans out of their current, lazy state of lethargy.

Those proposals call for every human being on earth to have a programmable biochip implanted at birth. This coded chip or "computer I.D." will, say federal officials and corporate planners, contain, as a minimum, biometrics data on the individual as conceived for *L.U.C.I.D.*

But, will a gullible public sit idly by while Big Brother cleverly rams this smooth battering ram into their chests? Larry Bates' excellent publication, *Monetary and Economic Review*, carried an article which appropriately describes our current predicament as free citizens about to be stripped of our liberties and dignity. The article, provocatively entitled, "Smart Cards: They Make Our Enslavement So Convenient," warns:

Remember, the goal of the New World Order crowd is to control the economic and social behavior of everyone. Many people will succumb to this financial slavery out of mere convenience.[21]

Paranoid Thinking...or Reality?

Whatever technology man can invent, the Illuminati, in the last days, will use to control and either pacify or induce fear and terror in the masses. Some may call this paranoid thinking, but the wise know it as truth. As *Media Bypass*, a patriotic magazine, in an article entitled, "A Chip in Your Shoulder," stated:

Implant technology is not new. Although routinely ridiculed as a paranoid delusion, the Food and Drug Administration (FDA) has mandated electronic biochip implants into humans receiving pacemakers, prosthetic devices, and even breast implants since 1994. Literally thousands of Americans now carry these microdevices under their skin...Endangered animals and livestock also carry implants to track their migration of feeding habits.[22]

Interestingly, Timothy McVeigh, alleged bomber of the federal building in Oklahoma City, claimed that, while on active duty, the U.S. Army implanted a "tracking device" in his body. Was it this device which allowed the federal Gestapo cops to track down and locate McVeigh so soon after the bombing incident? Did the feds know where the suspected terrorist was at all times, courtesy of an overflying satellite—even *before* the bomb went off?

Dr. Rod Lewis, publisher of *CE Chronicles* and head of a scientific study network in Houston, Texas, apparently mindful of this distinct possibility, noted: "There are no reports that McVeigh had any type of mental illness, disorder, or displayed any clinical symptoms of paranoid or delusional thinking."[23]

Lewis further raises eyebrows when he writes:

What makes this case even more interesting is that D. Louis J. West, M.D., Professor of Psychiatry at UCLA, was interviewed on CNN the day after the bombing as an expert on "terrorist behavior."

Dr. West was the examining psychiatrist of Jack Ruby, assassin of Lee Harvey Oswald. He is also well known for his work in mind control in the 1960s and was a proponent of the use of biochip implantation to control violence.

It has been rumored that much of Dr. West's research was funded by the Central Intelligence Agency. It is now known that Dr. West will be the consulting psychiatrist for the case and that all of Mr. McVeigh's military and medical records have been closed.

Dr. West's name has been mentioned in a number of books about mind control including Jim Keith's *A Casebook on Alternative 3*, Walter Bowarts' *Operation Mind Control*, and Martin Cannon's white paper, "The Controllers."

Is it just coincidence that of all the psychiatrists in the United States, Dr. West would be selected to oversee the psychiatric evaluation of Mr. McVeigh? It seems that in the eyes of the government there was good reason— something that they did not want others to see perhaps?[24]

Chicago Tribune

Chicago Sports Final
50¢ Newsstand

Tuesday, May 7, 1996

Chicago Tribune

A TRIBUNE PUBLISHING COMPANY
435 N. MICHIGAN AVE., CHICAGO, ILL. 60611

Tribune retail stores
Visit our retail outlets for back issues of the paper, to order copies of photos or complete pages from the Tribune and to request permission to reprint stories.

CHICAGO ....(312) 222-3080

In future, tiny chip may get under skin

Critics argue device invites Big Brother

By Jon Van
TRIBUNE STAFF WRITER

A tiny chip implanted inside the human body to send and receive radio messages, long a popular delusion among paranoids, is likely to be marketed as a consumer item early in the next century.

Several technologies already available or under development will enable electronics firms to make implantable ID locators, say futurists, and our yearning for convenience and security makes them almost irresistible to marketers.

"This is currently very hot," said Edward Cornish, president of the World Future Society, based in Bethesda, Md. "The field is developing because the technology is becoming available to do it."

He added: "Its appeal will depend on what features are offered and the price. I'm sure a large number of people would want such products."

Inevitably, implantable radio locators conjure up visions of Big Brother and unscrupulous scientists abusing such technology to control the masses. But the researchers laying the foundations for this technology see their work as helping humankind, not subverting privacy.

They seek to aid people using wireless phones to summon emergency help, to track soldiers who become lost on maneuvers and to enable people to get along without carrying cash by automatically crediting an account.

Animal advocates already urge pet owners to have tiny identification chips implanted in their dogs and cats so if they are lost, shelters can identify them through a national computerized database.

The notion of using implantable chips to control humans isn't entirely absent, even in these early stages of the technology's development.

Cornish noted that authorities have experimented for years with fitting con-

See CHIPS, PAGE 16

A10-■ Sunday, April 2, 1989 Marin Independent Journal

Future shocker: 'Biochip'

'Science fiction' technology here

By Teresa Allen
IJ senior writer

Don't reach for your wallet at the check-out counter.

After your food items have been priced, tallied and bagged, simply pass your hand over the computer code scanner used on the groceries, and the bill will be automatically deducted from your checking account.

Or consider this: A powerful "biochip" made from living protein that, once surgically implanted in the brain, could make it possible to program or "upload" an unlimited amount of information into the mind — without having ever cracked open a book.

Impossible? The plot of a science fiction novel?

The technology to accomplish such fantastic feats is already here or, as in the case of the living biochip, in the process of being developed, says Tim Willard, executive officer of the World Future Society, a Washington D.C.-based organization that claims 27,000 members worldwide, including _____ "think" au-

Chip used with cattle, swine

The microchip targeted for use by the humane society is made by Destron/IDI firm in Colorado and marketed by Info-pet of Southern California. Already the chip is being used to track the health history of swine and cattle, identify race horses in Europe and monitor the migration pattern of salmon in the Northwest, according to Destron President Jim Seiler.

In another fisheries application, salmon injected with the chip are scanned as they pass through dam sites "to assure environmentalists they are not being chewed up in the (dam) turbines," Seiler said.

Other applications could include identifying pets for health insurance purposes and identifying animal research subjects in lieu of clipping ears and toes.

While there are "10,000 ideas to explore" when it comes to the chip's potential, Seiler said Destron is only concerned with animal identification and is not considering human application.

See Future, back page

Future

From page A1

"There's no need to (apply the technology to humans)," he said. "The human fingerprint is unique. Animals don't have a unique identifier."

But Willard, managing editor of the World Future Society's bi-monthly magazine called Futurist, said the technology behind such a microchip is "fairly uncomplicated" and with a little refinement, could be used in a variety of human applica-

The Marin Independent Journal (USPS 435-590) is published Monday through Friday and Saturday and Sunday mornings by California Newspapers Inc. (Second-class postage paid at Novato, CA and additional mailing offices. POSTMASTER: Send address changes to Marin Independent Journal, P.O. Box 6150, Novato, CA 94948) General office 1012 Lincoln Ave., San Rafael CA 94915. (415) 883-8600. In Southern Marin, call toll free (415) 381-3327

Peter A. Harvtz — Publisher
Gary Shan — Associate Publisher
Joy Streichman — Managing Editor
Bruce Emley — Circulation Director
Roland Keller — Advertising Director
Jon Jensen — Marketing Director
Lottie B. Carr — Personnel Director
Frank J. Newfield — Personnel Services Director
Glenn D. Bennetts — Production Director — Controller

381 2712
381 7358
382 2770
382 2710
381 2211
382 2217
382 2308
382 2302
382 7262
382 7228

"People tend to be romantic about their independence and privacy, but the reality is that most information pertaining to education, credit history, whatever, is readily available to just about anyone who asks. Anyone who has ever gone through a credit check knows this."

Another futurist found the concept of microchip imp____

Science is on the threshold of perfecting the ultimate means of human control—the implantable, reprogrammable biochip.

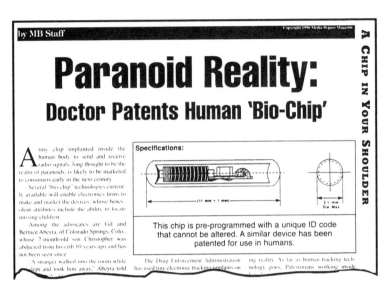

Paranoid Reality:

Doctor Patents Human 'Bio-Chip'

A CHIP IN YOUR SHOULDER

A tiny chip implanted inside the human body to send and receive radio signals, long thought to be the realm of paranoids, is likely to be marketed to consumers early in the next century.

Several "bio-chip" technologies currently available will enable electronics firms to make and market the devices, whose benevolent attributes include the ability to locate missing children.

Among the advocates are Gil and Bernice Abeyta, of Colorado Springs, Colo., whose 7-month-old son Christopher was abducted from his crib 10 years ago and has not been seen since.

"A stranger walked into the room while [he] slept and took him away," Abeyta told

The Drug Enforcement Administration has used tiny electronic tracking implants on

ing reality. As far as human-tracking technology goes, Palestinians working inside

Specifications:

This chip is pre-programmed with a unique ID code that cannot be altered. A similar device has been patented for use in humans.

Media Bypass magazine reports that biochips are real and not a paranoid delusion.

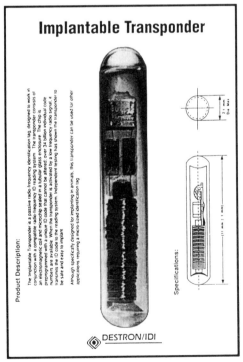

This implantable transponder is marketed by Destron/IDI Corporation.

•••• THE CHARLOTTE OBSERVER Sunday, May 22, 1994 **9B**

Dr. Tom Watson and assistant Belinda Higginbotham scan Eli after he received a microchip. The chip is used as an identification system that can protect a pet even if its tags are lost.

DIANNE V. CURTAIN/Staff

Gaston pound gets chip ID system

New scanner will help find owners of pets with microchips

By CHRIS HAGEN
Staff Writer

GASTONIA — It's been two weeks since Kevin Campbell's floppy-eared hound Gracie ran away, but the pain of her disappearance lingers.

"It has been a constant frustration," said Campbell, of Dallas, N.C. "I have called the pound every day and spent many hours searching the woods for her, but have no positive idea where she could be."

Soon, there will be help for ~ton pet owners such as Camp-

Charlotte veterinary hospitals have been using the chip for months, but it's just now coming to Gaston County, veterinarians say. So far, vets say, about 40 Gaston pet owners have had animals chipped.

The chip, which costs between $31 and $38, is available at Wilkinson Animal Hospital and All Creatures Pet Hospital.

Pets suffer little from the procedure, vets said.

Tagged pets are registered with the company that makes the chip, American Veterinar~ ~dentifica-

they dug a hole under his backyard fence and took off across rush-hour traffic.

"I did not think it would ever happen to me because they were older and well-trained and because they were in a big fenced-in backyard," he said.

Neighbor Terri Vass found the two dogs later, shaken and scared.

Campbell's hound Gracie is still missing. Campbell, a water treatment plant operator, bought Gracie and another hound, Joe, as puppies.

He'd ~

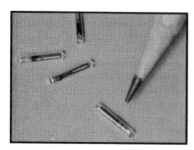
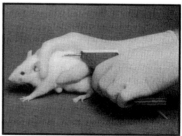

Implantable chips are said to be the answer to missing or stolen pets and animals. Some cities and towns now require all owners to have the devices implanted in the bodies of their pets.

Implantable biochips are getting smaller and more powerful. At right, a laboratory mouse has a biochip injected into its body.

Whether or not Timothy McVeigh has (or had?) a biochip implanted on his body—and I suspect he did—we still must face up to the chilling fact that, with the implementation of *Project L.U.C.I.D.*, a tiny, implantable, programmable, biochip computer lies awaiting in our future. The inevitable is at hand. Allen Woodham, head of *South East Christian Witness,* a prophetic ministry based in Australia, accurately says that each of us must confront the hideous reality which has now raised its ugly head:

As you read this, electronic transponder implants are being introduced worldwide in the animal-control industry. They are considered an improvement, and no doubt they are. But someday soon, the offshoots of this system will be used in a way that their inventors probably never envisioned: Satan's "Big Brother," New World Order, global government.

Currently, Americans are numbered with a nine-digit Social Security number that allows them to be tracked anywhere in the country with computers. Soon, however, this system will be replaced by a new, global, 18-digit mesh-block configuration of international numbers that will allow people to be tracked internationally.

Such a planetary network will enable the Illuminati's New World Order, United Nations-controlled world government to assign everyone on earth a specific and unique I.D. number for tracking and control. This 18-digit numbering system will consist of THREE separate sets of SIX DIGITS each: 6-6-6!

Coincidental? No. Not if you believe Bible prophecy.

Implanting that number just beneath the skin of the right hand, as the Bible foretells in Revelation 13:16-18, is now a practical reality! Individuals so numbered readily could be identified, tracked, controlled, and "skip-traced" in all their movements and activities anywhere in the world!

This technology undoubtedly will lead to a universal system of totalitarian enslavement under a computerized, global, economic network of electronic bondage. In this soon-coming CASHLESS ELECTRONIC DEBIT system, no one will be able to BUY OR SELL anything, anywhere without the New World Order global biochip "MARK" in their right hands or foreheads (the mark of the Beast).

The biochip will be the agency by which all financial transactions are registered. Without it, no transactions of any kind will be permitted; there will be no income, no food, no shelter. Once in place universally, Satan's system of total electronic enslavement will have been imposed upon all the citizens of the New World Order. No one will be excluded from having to take his "MARK" without facing the death penalty...a truly "DO or DIE" situation![25]

My good friend, Allen Woodham, is right on target with his comments and concerns. I'm quite sure that after

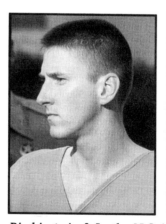

Biochip twins? In the U.S.A., accused Oklahoma City bomber Timothy McVeigh complained that the U.S. Army implanted a computer chip in his buttocks. In England, in 1995, a Buckingham Palace spokesman said that young Prince William, heir to the British Throne, had a microchip implanted somewhere in his anatomy to discourage would-be kidnappers.

reading this book, *Project L.U.C.I.D.*, he will be more convinced than ever that the advent of this dark technology and the establishment of the massive, behemoth, global computer network conceived for *L.U.C.I.D.* net presents mankind with a "Do or Die" predicament.

Prophetic Insight Needed

Regrettably, the great majority of Americans and other world citizens will perish because they do not possess the prophetic knowledge and foresight necessary for survival.

George Orwell, in *1984*, his classic novel of Big Brother and a coming, totalitarian state, observed that very few people are awake and alert to the machinations and manipulations of the controllers. Thus, the people, as a whole, fall victim to a colossal conspiracy out of ignorance and because of apathy and denial of reality:

> The people could be made to accept the most flagrant violations of reality, because they never fully grasped the enormity of what was demanded of them, and were not sufficiently interested in public events to notice what was happening.[26]

How thrilling and lifesaving is Bible prophecy! Those who trust in God's Word have a tremendous advantage over the multiplied herds of "simple" (that is, ignorant, deceived, scripture-denying) people. The discerning person who relies on the Bible sees evil coming in advance and wisely finds protection under the wings of the Most High. As it is recorded, "A prudent man foreseeth the evil, and hideth himself: but the simple pass on, and are punished" (Proverbs 22:3).

FIVE

Mystery Mark of the New Age

Will the implantable biochip, linked in with the *L.U.C.I.D.* worldwide control net, become the basis for the mysterious, but diabolical, Mark of the Beast? It seems possible, even likely, that this will prove to be the case. But, as we shall see, the elitists who now control the U.S. government and the United Nations also have other technological systems on the horizon in store for us which could set up the mark system.

Martin Anderson, a former Reagan aide who's now a Senior Fellow at the Hoover Research Institute at Stanford University in Palo Alto, California, is among those who have taken the lead in warning the public about the threat to our individual privacy and security by such high tech tools as Smart I.D. Cards and biochip implants. In an article published in the *San Jose Mercury News* which was syndicated nationally, Anderson stated: "Unless this move to force a national identity card on Americans is stopped quickly, we may live to see the end of privacy in the United States. All of us will be tagged like so many fish."[1]

In *The Washington Times*, Martin Anderson further escalated his warning of the encroaching danger when he cautioned Americans *not* to believe the rosy predictions of the politicians and bureaucrats that the proposed I.D. card biochip implant would make life nicer, more convenient, and safer for the citizenry. In ominous tones,

Anderson said that exactly the opposite will occur:

> This tiny microchip transponder is sort of like a *Technological Tattoo*, and far more effective than the numbers the Nazis marked indelibly on the arms of concentration camp victims...
>
> There is no difference in principle between being forced to carry a microchip in a plastic I.D. card in your wallet or in a little transponder pellet injected into your arm. The principle that Big Brother has the right to *track* you is inherent in both. The only thing that differentiates the two techniques is a layer of your skin.[2]

Anderson's conclusions in his timely article sound a remarkable warning to us. "Once you denigrate the idea of privacy," Anderson observed, "all kinds of innovative government controls are possible, things that didn't even occur to Aldous Huxley when he wrote his chilling novel, *Brave New World.*"[3]

Reagan Shelves Idea For I.D. Cards

It was also Martin Anderson who, in his book, *Revolution*, revealed that during the Reagan administration of the '80s, several top cabinet officials were urging President Ronald Reagan to implement a computerized national I.D. card. The rationale for the proposal was that such a system would help put a lid on illegal immigration.[4]

But Anderson, who at the time was a domestic advisor to the President and sat in on this particular cabinet meeting, spoke up and gave the group something to think about.

"I would like to suggest another way that I think is a lot better," he told them, serious in demeanor but clearly being facetious. "It's a lot cheaper, it can't be counterfeited. It's very lightweight, and it's impossible to lose. It's even waterproof."[5]

"All we have to do," Anderson continued, "is tattoo

an identification number on the inside of everybody's arm."[6]

Anderson, of course, was being tongue-in-cheek about the I.D. tattoos. His reference was to the tattooing of numbers on victims in Nazi concentration camps. Survivors still bear the dreaded tattoo markings to this day. But his point came across loud and clear.

Mr. Anderson described the stunned reaction of those present: "There were several gasps around the table. A couple of the cabinet members looked as if they had been slapped. No one said anything for a long time."[7]

Interior Secretary James Watt then brought up an implication he felt important to conservative Christians: I.D. tattoos are considered the Mark of the Beast (the Antichrist) mentioned in Revelation 13:16-18. Some Christians also look on government I.D. cards as a first step toward I.D. tattoos. Conservative Christians, Watt noted, formed a crucial foundation for Mr. Reagan's electoral success.

Ronald Reagan, a consummately wise politician who professed a belief in Bible prophecy, caught the implication. He then hushed the cabinet and efficiently dismissed the I.D. card proposal by sardonically remarking, "Maybe we should just brand all the babies."[8]

"A Chip in Your Ear"

The proposal for a national I.D. card system never came up again during the Reagan White House administration. But in 1993, with the election of Bill Clinton as President of the of the United States, a campaign was begun in earnest to propagandize and push the American people to accept the high tech, electronically velvetized handcuffs of I.D. cards and biochips.

One Clinton advisor promoting the biochip "mark" is Dr. Mary Jane England, a member of Hillary Clinton's ill-fated, socialized, national healthcare initiative. Addressing a conference sponsored by computer giant IBM in Palm Springs, California, in 1994, England not only endorsed the proposed mandatory national I.D. Smart Card, but went one scary leap further:

> The smart card is a wonderful idea, but even better would be the capacity not to have a card, and I call it "a chip in your ear," that would actually access your medical records, so that no matter where you were, even if you came into an emergency room unconscious, we would have some capacity to access that medical record. We need to go beyond the narrow conceptualization of the smart card and really use some of the technology that's out there.[9]

Don't think for a moment that only Clinton clones and liberal democrats are behind the sinister drive to mark and brand us with numbers, enslave us through technological tattoos, and track us with computerized, all seeing eye systems. Satan is not a registered Democrat; he's more than happy to operate through the auspices of the Republican Party, too. Witness the discussion around the presidential cabinet conference table during the Reagan era.

One Republican Party stalwart who's been actively stumping for a national I.D. card system is California Governor Pete Wilson. Wilson has repeatedly echoed the liberal democrat call for mandatory I.D. Smart Cards. Wilson, like so many others, conjures up the straw man of the pervasive immigration problem. An I.D. card system is needed to stem illegal immigration, says the governor, who is joined in his hypocritical campaign for mandatory I.D. cards by California's Democratic Party Senators Diane Feinstein and Barbara Boxer.[10]

But, is the immigration crisis just a convenient excuse for Big Brother to use to clamp down on our personal rights and liberties? Enriqueta Ramos, an Orange County Community College (Los Angeles) official, sounded a legitimate warning when asked about the proposal of Wilson, Feinstein, and Boxer. "A national identity card could lead California down a dangerous path," Ramos

The Washington Times

| Washington | October 11, 1993 | DC |

MARTIN ANDERSON

High-tech national tattoo

The high-tech national identity card that President Clinton has proposed as part of his radical health care legislation is an ingenious device for keeping track of the personal lives of Americans.

This identity card is designed to keep permanent, accessible records of all aspects of your health care, including the details of every doctor visit, every drugstore prescription and every hospital treatment.

The card could be used to crack down on welfare fraud, trace deadbeat dads who refuse to pay child support, supplant our Social Security cards, our draft cards and our passports, maybe even to register voters and control voting fraud.

The uses will be limited, not by technology, but only by the imagination of government officials and their respect for our privacy.

Cost is not a serious problem. A state-of-the-art identity card can be manufactured, in quantity, for a dollar or two each.

To make this tracking system work, every one of us must have a

"Don't leave home without it !"

The national identity card will become so ubiquitous, so necessary in order to comply with government regulations, that we will be obliged to carry it with us at all times. That leads to a serious problem.

What if we lose it? Can anyone who finds the card or who steals it get access to the information?

Well, we could wear the card on a chain around our necks, the way security passes are safeguarded in military installations and inside the White House. But that is a bit tacky and, in the eyes of some, demeaning.

There is another solution, although I hesitate to mention the idea because one of Mr. Clinton's White House aides may tak........

Sort of like a technological tattoo, and far more efficacious than the numbers that the Nazis marked indelibly on the inner forearms of concentration camp prisoners.

True, an implanted transponder can't yet hold anywhere near as much material as a smart card. But if the desire is there, larger size implants and tiny microchips could soon increase its data storage capacity.

Of course, most Americans will find a surgically implanted government microchip repugnant. At least for the foreseeable future, the use of this ingenious device will be confined to its current use: the tracking of dogs

President Bill Clinton tried to bamboozle the American public into accepting a national, Smart I.D. Card system under the guise of universal healthcare services. In The Washington Times, Martin Anderson warned of a "high tech national tattoo."

was quoted as saying. "It will create a neo-Nazi state in the United States where we will be required to tell on each other. Next thing you know, we'll have tattoos on our bodies."[11]

A Planetary Dictator's Dream

Ramos and others who oppose mandatory I.D. cards and human control, mark systems, wisely see these intrusive, privacy-destroying devices as a throwback to the Nazi era and to its savagely brutal concentration camps. But we should never forget that the Leninists and Stalinists of Communist Russia and its captive republics were equally brutal and bloody, if not more so. The Soviet Union had its I.D. cards—and the "new" Russia still does today! The same is true for Maoist Red China, and for today's supposedly more enlightened Chinese People's Republic.

Throughout history, all tyrants, of whatever political stripe or ideology, have desired the power and Big Brother control that I.D. cards provide. But in the past, the monstrous dictators and mass murderers had only low tech methods to assist in their bloody operations. Now, however, as we near the 21st century, science has engineered the *L.U.C.I.D.* net, introduced the implantable biochip, and promises soon to give us other, advanced control systems. How blissfully thrilled a modern-day Hitler, Lenin, Stalin, or Mao Tse Tung would be to arm his henchmen with such uniquely marvelous high tech toys—toys able to identify, track, and zap the beleaguered, state-owned slaves of the increasingly global plantation.

The National Security Agency's *Project L.U.C.I.D.*, with all its technological wizardry, is a future, planetary dictator's dream—and a Christian and national patriot's nightmare. Someday, the Holy Bible prophesies, that planetary dictator will emerge on the scene, lusting for blood, and energized to do his dirty work by the devils who possess him.

The world is being prepared at this very moment for the arrival of the Antichrist, and, if current trends hold, the gloomy day of his ascension to power will not be too long in coming.

The Antichrist to Lead a One World Government

Perhaps the most frightening and chilling passage in scripture is Revelation 13, which describes the rise to power of the bloodthirsty Beast, the Antichrist whose number is 666. The Bible reveals that this false "Christ" will blaspheme against God and that he will "make war with the saints" and overcome them. It prophesies: "All that dwell upon the earth shall worship him, whose names are not written in the book of life of the Lamb slain from the foundation of the world" (Revelation 13:8).

I am convinced that we are on the threshold of seeing this Beast of Revelation astonishingly come to power. We know that as soon as he has taken over the reigns of a One World Government, he will begin to savagely persecute those who refuse to kneel to Satan. Bible prophesy declares that the Antichrist and his false prophet, the world religious leader who serves him, shall have an image of the Beast set up in all churches, synagogues, and temples around the world. Every person will then be forced to worship the image of the Beast...or they shall be killed (Revelation 13:15).

The New Age Antichrist will enforce his iron rule by requiring every man, woman, and child on planet earth to take a hideous Mark:

> And he causeth all, both small and great, rich and poor, free and bond, to receive a mark in their right hand, or in their foreheads. And that no man might buy or sell, save he that had the mark, or the name of the beast, or the number of his name. (Revelation 13:16-17)

In my #1 national bestselling book, *Mystery Mark of the New Age*, I uncovered the incredible, even mind-boggling, hidden Plan of the Illuminati and its occultic leaders to carry out Satan's orders by giving every one of us this dark and repugnant Mark. Revelation 13 *will* come to pass.

Mystery Mark of the New Age is a shocking exposé of this hidden Plan to give all the Mark of the Beast. In the book I quote many of the most prominent leaders in the New Age and lay bare their remarkable, yet brutal, design for world domination.

Mystery Mark of the New Age fully explains what the Bible tells us about both the image and the Mark of the Beast. In it, you'll discover that some New Agers have already taken the Mark! And you'll learn just how Satan's One World Religion plans to get every one of us to willingly take the heinous Mark.

No, the Beast will not have to force the world at gunpoint to worship him. If the dark New Age plan succeeds, every person on our planet will actually cherish the Mark that is to be given in their right hand or in their forehead. They will desperately desire it, and even line up by the thousands at churches converted into New Age worship centers, just for the glorious opportunity to take the Mark.

Yes, I know—this is all so bizarre. After all, who in their right mind would *knowingly* take a Mark that will doom them to everlasting hellfire and destruction?

> ...If any man worship the beast and his image, and receive his mark in his forehead, or in his hand, The same shall drink of the wine of the wrath of God, which is poured out without mixture into the cup of his indignation; and he shall be tormented with fire and brimstone in the presence of the holy angels, and in the presence of the Lamb. And the smoke of their torment ascendeth up for ever and ever... (Revelation 14:9-11)

Still, the majority are ignorant of their fate and will take the Mark. Bible prophecy *will* prove true. The truth of prophecy is even now being borne out. We are being *conditioned* by the masters of New Age propaganda and mind control. Satanic symbols, such as the unholy triangle and the pentagram star, are flooding our TV screens; they're in magazines and newspapers and on the covers of rock albums. *Mankind is being alchemically mind-warped with a new "paradigm shift" and is being readied for the New Age Kingdom!*

The corporate chieftains are aiding and abetting the cause of Antichrist, sometimes unwittingly, sometimes not. Take, for example, a recent advertisement by *MasterCard*, the international credit card firm. In *Colorado Christian News*, editor Joann Chiarello Bruso recently penned an article entitled, "Big Brother is Here." Her comments were eye-opening, to say the least:

> We knew it was coming. We've been talking about it for years. We've debated what it would look like, how it would be sold and implemented. Yet, somehow it seems too soon. Last month while in Arizona, Andrew, my son-in-law, saw a very interesting commercial. Just before we went to press, this same commercial was being aired in Colorado. A woman is pictured in an empty white room. As numbers whiz by her head you hear them being read: *social security, checking account, credit card, drivers license, health policy, telephone, fax, etc.*

> A voice asks, "How can you remember them all?" Then it declares, "Master Card is working on the solution. The one-digit pin."

> The camera focuses on the back of the woman's right hand; she flips it over and you see a close-up of her index finger with a pattern of dots. The voice-over states, *"Your personal mark."* It then proudly announces, Master Card will bring this to you in the future!

> Wow, what marketing strategy! A new mark solving the problem of remembering all those numbers. Lost or stolen cards become a problem of the past. Just scan your finger and, instantly, vital information is recorded

and decoded. Andrew said he about fell out of his chair when he saw the "mark" commercial. Although, all the signs indicate we are not too far away from this technology, Andrew didn't expect to see an advertisement for the personal mark during prime time TV.[12]

666 a Holy and Sacred Number?

As I point out in *Mystery Mark of the New Age*, occultic New Age leaders have even begun to tell the masses that 666 is a "holy and sacred number." They are encouraging us to create an image in our minds of a false god or goddess *and to worship that image*. Worse, they glowingly speak of the *coming great initiation* of all mankind into the Mystery Religion of the New Age. The culmination of this initiation, they say, is the taking of a Mark. Then, after receiving the Mark, these false teachers claim, you will become a divine god.

I cannot possibly describe to you how my heart sank when, through God's help, I first began to unravel this almost unimaginable and terrible Plan.

The fact that technology now makes possible the ultimate means of control of humanity predicted by *Revelation* is a clear indication that the Antichrist is about to make his move. His days of global conquest are at hand:

> And I saw, and behold a white horse: and he that sat on him had a bow; and a crown was given unto him: and he went forth conquering, and to conquer. (Revelation 6:2)

This passage in the sixth chapter of the book of *Revelation* is filled with prophetic significance. Here we see pictured the dreaded four horsemen of the apocalypse. First, the man on the white horse, followed in rapid succession by the riders of the red, black, and pale horses. These bring savage wars, death, famine, pestilence, disease, environmental and other grotesque horrors. This is the image of the global terror, spoil, and bloodshed that is to occur in the last days just prior to Jesus' glorious return.

Enter a Savior: The Man on the White Horse

Note that the first rider comes on a *white horse*. This indicates that he is to be almost universally admired as a peacemaker, a savior, who comes to *rescue humanity* from the severe crises and insoluble problems which confront us. Certainly today, our planet is besieged on every side. We have ethic strife and religious "cleansing" in Bosnia; street gangs and violence in many cities; cocaine, heroine, and other illegal drugs rampant everywhere; and the spread of the deadly AIDS epidemic. There is also sporadic terrorist activity in Israel and Lebanon and arrogant posturing and brutal suppression of captive republics in Russia. Meanwhile, many parts of Africa are gripped by anarchy, tribal hatreds, and starvation.

Japanese stock market and real estate values have collapsed. In Europe, the economic slump is threatening to turn into a tragic depression. Financial chaos is on the horizon. In the U.S.A. people fear that the federal budget deficit, looming like a malignant bogeyman, is going to seize the average American wage earner by the throat and drown us all in a sea of debt.[14]

Most of these crises are *created* by rogue governments, especially in America by the FBI, the NSA, the CIA, the BATF, and other alphabet agencies that secretly fund and sponsor domestic terrorism, Communist cells, neo-Nazi and KKK-type groups.

Domestic terrorism, especially, is the government created bugaboo expected to drive the frightened masses into the waiting arms of a Big Brother-styled government. I have presented ample evidence in the past—for example, in my videos *Fascist Terror Stalking America* and *The Bloodstained Hands of Big Brother Government*—that the United States' alphabet police, Gestapo establishment, under NSA supervision, runs virtually all the world's terrorist units. The World Trade Center bombing in New York City, the Oklahoma City massacre, and many others were planned and executed by government henchmen.[15]

The result was predictable: a media-generated outcry from Congress and the White House to pass so-called "Anti-Terrorist" legislation. This process, Bob Trefz writes in *Cherith Chronicle*, is called "Setting Up the Noose." He explains how it works:

> The way the noose works is this. The Anti-terrorism bill provides draconian measures against those alleged to fit the category of terrorism (or dissenters—those who might differ from the tyranny of administration), providing detention or deportation for those categorized or labeled as "aliens." The Biometric National ID card identifies by fingerprints, retina scans, and/or DNA every person in the nation.
>
> This provides the possibility of positive identification and tracking of all citizens for the enforcement of the Mark of the Beast. Those who *submit* to the Biometric ID can be required to submit all kinds of information in the process of qualifying as "citizens." Those who refuse to submit can be immediately identified as "aliens," noncitizens, dissenters, subject to *detention* or *deportation*.
>
> To those who know the history of the development of the Medieval and Spanish Inquisitions and of the modern twentieth century history of the Gestapo inquisition and of Hitler's path to power, today's parallels with the consolidation of police powers in the Third Reich are uncanny and profound. The personal road of the Jew to the detention and death camps began with *registration*. Now it looms on the horizon, very closely, in America.
>
> We are in the times analogous to the days of Hitler's bully boy storm-trooper attacks on dissidents as across this nation innocent people's homes are being raided, with possessions searched and stolen on a continuous

basis. We are in the days analogous to the Enabling Acts, and seizure of power of the executive, while the national police force is consolidated.[16]

With the government generating chaos and setting the noose, and under such austere and hostile circumstances as we currently face, men and women everywhere are crying out for a leader, a hero, a statesman to put things right—*a man on a white horse*. And many, inspired by an Illuminati-controlled press, are demanding that he be at the helm of a global organization.

Revelation tells us that the man on the white horse has a *bow:* He has the *military means* to make war to enforce the peace. We also see that he is given a *crown*. Thus, he shall be accorded the *political power* necessary to fulfill his global role as a conqueror.

The final steps in the prophetic puzzle have been set for the rider of the white horse to come forward and take his ominous place as the most evil man in the annals of human history. The planet and its people have been brainwashed, dumbed-down, and conditioned. They're ready. It's time.

The United Nations Plot

The United Nations has become center stage for the dramatic events now unfolding. Its Secretary-General, Egypt's Boutros Boutros-Ghali, has asked that the UN be given its own *World Army*. Global peace, says Boutros-Ghali, can only come from the mouth of a gun and from the fiery exhaust of an aircraft missile.

Calls have rung out from across the globe, imploring the UN to use its armed might and firepower to put down local insurgencies, rebellions, and violations. Somalia must be fed, Iraq tamed, Angola pacified, Bosnia's cleansing stopped, and South Africa cured of its racial divisions.

Some have suggested the UN send its blue berets into Los Angeles, Chicago, Houston, and other U.S. cities in the event of race or other riots. The claim is that local law enforcement cannot be trusted.

In Rio de Janeiro, environmental activists at the Earth Summit demanded that the rich nations extract billions in taxes from their citizenry. The money would go into UN coffers and be doled out to Third World nations whose environments have supposedly been polluted by the U.S. and other Western nations. The UN is also to be given authority to police the world, acting across national borders, punishing polluters and levying fines on "guilty," global citizens. Yes, UN forces must become the enviro-cops of planet earth.

World Army for UN in Sight

The clamor for the United Nations to get its own, permanent World Army is reaching epidemic proportions. First, UN Secretary-General Boutros-Ghali went public in *Foreign Affairs*, the Council on Foreign Relations' propagandistic journal, with the plan for a UN force. Then George Bush pitched in to help by committing U.S. troops to Somalia *under UN auspices*.

None other than the Great Communicator himself, the former President, and now ailing, Ronald Reagan, was ordered by the Secret Brotherhood of the Illuminati to make propaganda speeches in favor of the UN's World Army. He kicked off his campaign at Oxford University in England on December 4th, 1993. Bill Clinton has also been enlisted to push for a UN standing military force. Meanwhile, New World Order puppet Mikhail Gorbachev continues to strut the UN line at every public appearance he makes.

Someday soon, unless the Secret Brotherhood is stopped, the UN's armed forces will be given total military control and enforcement power for all of planet earth. It is planned by the elite that America's own, once proud Army, Navy, Air Force, Marines, and Coast Guard become mere branches and attachés of a new, global, peacekeeping network. The leaders of the Secret Brotherhood's mighty arsenal will be in full command, and America's Constitution will be as dead as a doorknob.

Too unbelievable to imagine, you say? Well friends, just watch and see. There *will* be a world government and army. I know, because God's prophetic Word says so (for example, Revelation 13 and 17).

Only the UN Can Do It

The world's problems seem to be insurmountable. Only a One World Government and even a unified new religion can suffice, say the "experts." Only a mighty, all conquering United Nations can get the job done. Thus it was, that in Fulton, Missouri in 1992, Russia's Mikhail Gorbachev proposed a global government be set up. Other world leaders quickly endorsed the idea.

In 1996, at Gorbachev's State of the World Forum at the inactivated Presidio Army Base, in San Francisco, similar cries for world government and world religion were heard. Significantly, one of the men who attended Gorbachev's bash was billionaire Bill Gates, founder of *Microsoft*, the corporation that will furnish the internet capability for *L.U.C.I.D.*

A Great Leader is Needed: The Antichrist

Naturally, this enhanced, more powerful UN, being structured as a One World Government, will need a *leader*, a great leader, a man eminently qualified to head up a global army, a planetary IRS, an international environmental police force, and a United Nations intelligence agency similar to America's infamous CIA and the U.S.S.R.'s notorious KGB. He will have to be a man who is authoritative, yet be willing to solicit and heed the advice of a *Council of Wise Men*.

Believe me, the elitists at the highest echelon of the

Microsoft Corporation founder Bill Gates, shown here on the cover of **Time** *magazine, attended Mikhail Gorbachev's State of the World Forum in San Francisco.*

The United Nations is being given the military power to punish resisters to the New World Order.

Illuminati have just the right man in mind for this new, all powerful position of *World Fuhrer*. Isn't that why their own in-house agency, the *Council on Foreign Relations (CFR)*, has adopted its strange, but revealing, logo: *A man riding a white horse?*

The CFR logo, as pictured in the organization's quarterly journal, *Foreign Affairs*, depicts a strong, virulent, naked rider atop a magnificent white steed. He aggressively stretches upward his right arm in a defiant demonstration of victory and triumph. But look at the mysterious hand gesture. Are the man's fingers symbolizing the occultic sign of the horned devil, *el diablo*, or is this a mere illusion?

A quarter of a century ago, European leader Henri Spaak, then the Secretary-General of NATO, in a moment of frustration and despair, blurted out, "We are tired of piecemeal solutions to our problems. Give us a man— whether he be devil or god—and we will follow him."

Now today, in these last fateful months before the seventh millennium, as we draw near to the year 2000 AD, Mr. Spaak's wish is on the threshold of coming to pass. The rider is about to mount the white horse. He will lead a strengthened and vigilant World Army, and he will preside over an organization, the United Nations,

This mysterious logo of a rider on a white horse is found on each issue of the CFR publication, Foreign Affairs.

which shall cast a piercing stare from its all seeing eye throughout the four corners of the globe.

The U.S. Constitution, our standard for more than two centuries, is quietly being set aside. The protests of American patriots are being scorned. The One World Government which the Illuminati has worked for and dreamed of is now in sight. The grand scheme of the Freemasons and their Bilderbergers Group is being crowned with success.

But listen closely: Can you hear it?—the echo of that tremendous voice that came to the apostle John on the Isle of Patmos so very long ago. The voice that once revealed a great, great mystery: *"Come and see...behold a pale horse; and his name that sat on him was Death, and Hell followed with him."* (Revelation 6)

The Only Means of Escape

Who can escape the Mark of the New Age Beast? The answer is revealed in the Scriptures: Only those who are sealed in their souls by the Holy Spirit of the Living God.

This is the message that Jesus Christ, our Saviour, wishes to convey to a lost world strongly deluded by the New Age, Illuminati lie. God's wish is that no one perish. He loves us so much that He gave His only begotten Son to die for our sins. But all who reject His love and rebel against His Word shall not escape the Beast and his Mark.

Please, go out into the byways and highways and compel all whom you meet to turn to Jesus. The hour surely is late. The Beast is even now slouching his way toward his final destiny. Like lost sheep, millions will follow the coming New Age Messiah to their doom. Yet, Jesus' momentous words still ring out across the centuries:

Verily, verily, I say unto you, He that heareth my word, and believeth on him that sent me, hath everlasting life, and shall not come into condemnation; but is passed from death unto life. (John 5:24)

SIX

ISO 9000: The Program to Mark All Mammon on Earth With the Supernatural Number of the Beast

No man can serve two masters," Jesus Christ said. "Ye cannot serve God and mammon" (Matthew 6:24). In setting forth this principle of governance, our Lord made clear the fact that higher things are of the Spirit, while worldly things—"*mammon*"—are of the Adversary. God is sovereign and has defeated the Adversary but, according to His will, He allows Satan to continue for a brief period of history. Thus, the Bible tells us that, until Christ returns, Satan is "god of this world." Only Christians are immune from his powers. He is temporarily master of earth and all its products and goods (its *mammon*) are controlled by the devil through his human agents.

How fitting, therefore, that the planet's elite overseers have come up with an incredible new system to minutely control all the world's mammon. Called *ISO 9000* certification, this system is enveloping every manufacturer and producer on earth. I believe the ISO 9000 program will greatly assist in the control of mankind's property and goods by Big Brother's universal *L.U.C.I.D.* net.

What do the numerals "9-0-0-0" signify? In occult numerology, *nine* is the ultimate number of evil. In the number nine is contained a concealed 666! Occult numerologists add the three digits 6, 6, and 6, to produce 18. Then, the digits 1 and 8, added, produce the number 9. Thus, the single number 9 conceals the triple number of the beast, 666.

The three 0s, in turn, would likely represent the unholy trinity of Satan—three open *circles,* or sun orbs.

Could, then, the coded ISO 9000 designation represent the 666 Beast's computerized system of identification of all the world's mammon, to which he claims exclusive title and ownership?

ISO 9000 Becomes the Universal Standard

Virtually every corporation in every industry is abuzz with talk of the mandatory ISO 9000 program. Soon, by the year 2000, it is expected that no one on the planet—whether a company or an individual—will be able to make and sell products without ISO 9000 approval and certification.

In *American Papermaker,* an industry journal, Jackie Cox writes: "ISO 9000 has become the minimum standard to do business in the worldwide marketplace of the 1990s and beyond."[1] Sue Jackson, consultant in the DuPont Corporation's Quality Management & Technology Center, adds: "ISO 9000 is the quality system certification that companies, whether they be mills or suppliers, will need to have if they are to do business in a unified Europe, the U.S., and worldwide."[2]

Already, over 100 countries have adopted the ISO 9000 standards as their own for quality control systems. ISO 9000 certification began in Europe as a result of a command decision made by the *Bilderbergers,* a secretive group of about 125 of the richest and most powerful industrialists and bankers on earth. At first, it was "voluntary." But current plans are, that by the end of 1999, it will become *mandatory.* ISO 9000 is fast becoming the sole requirement for conducting commerce in all nations of the world.

The super rich fully intend to drive every entrepreneur and product maker—small and great—out of business who does not go along with their plan for *registration* of all who produce goods, or mammon, on earth. This brings to mind the prophecy found in Revelation 18, which chronicles the fall of *commercial* Mystery Babylon:

> And he cried mightily with a strong voice, saying, Babylon the great is fallen, is fallen, and is become the habitation of devils, and the hold of every foul spirit, and a cage of every unclean and hateful bird.

> And the merchants of the earth shall weep and mourn over her; for no man buyeth their merchandise any more:

> The merchandise of gold, and silver, and precious stones, and of pearls, and fine linen, and purple, and silk, and scarlet, and all thyine wood, and all manner vessels of ivory, and all manner vessels of most precious wood, and of brass, and iron, and marble,

> And cinnamon, and odours, and ointments, and frankincense, and wine, and oil, and fine flour, and wheat, and beasts, and sheep, and horses, and chariots, and slaves, and souls of men.

> And the fruits that thy soul lusted after are departed from thee, and all things which were dainty and goodly are departed from thee, and thou shalt find them no more at all.

> The merchants of these things, which were made rich by her, shall stand afar off for the fear of her torment, weeping and wailing,

> And saying, Alas, alas, that great city, that was clothed in fine linen, and purple, and scarlet, and decked with gold, and precious stones, and pearls!

> For in one hour so great riches is come to nought. And every shipmaster, and all the company in ships, and

sailors, and as many as trade by sea, stood afar off,

And cried when they saw the smoke of her burning, saying, What city is like unto this great city!

And they cast dust on their heads, and cried, weeping and wailing, saying, Alas, alas, that great city, wherein were made rich all that had ships in the sea by reason of her costliness! for in one hour is she made desolate. (Revelation 18: 2, 11-19)

Thus, we see that the end-times, universal, *free trade* commercial system is not "free" at all. It is controlled. ISO 9000 will guarantee this control. As one, top industry expert attests:

Governmental agencies are adopting the ISO 9000 standards as their own quality system standards. The U.S. Department of Defense (DOD), NATO, and the FDA have all announced their intention to adopt ISO 9000, *possibly with some additional requirements.*[3]

Computer Internet Registration Required

A knowledgeable DOD procurement director, a friend of mine, confided privately to me that, "Through EDI/EC (Electronic Commerce)/Internet, the federal government has stated that *all* business transactions must be done electronically through the internet by the year 2000."

Moreover, my friend adds that, "The federal government will soon require all contractors to be *registered* in the CCR *(Centralized Contractor Registration)* System."

This, he says, means that all persons and companies doing business with the government must register, be issued, and use a TPN *(Trading Partner Number)*.

"If they don't have this *number*," he warns, "they will *not* be allowed to sell their products—period!"

Imagine! Whether you produce a bookshelf, a screw,

a watch, a hammer, or a trash can, you'll be squeezed out of the marketplace *unless* your manufacturing or production "facility"—even if it's your garage or home workshop—receives the ISO 9000 *mark* of certification. Even then, you'll still need to be registered and have a "Trading Partner Number (TPN)." Moreover, you'll be required to register your number and identify all your transactions by use of the global, internet computer system. That's the same system where we find *L.U.C.I.D.* net!

Large or small, every producer must fall in line, bringing to pass the Bible's forecast that the Beast, "causeth all, both small and great, rich and poor, free and bond, to receive a mark...And that no man might buy or sell, save he that had the mark, or the name of the beast, or the number of his name" (Revelation 13:16-17).

Rudolph G. Boznak, with the international management consulting firm of United Research, Inc., writing in *Industrial Engineering* magazine, tells of one international computer manufacturer who "painfully discovered" that because of ISO 9000, $1.5 billion of his European sales were at risk."[4] This corporation was threatened: Obtain ISO 9000 certification for your products, or you're out!

Meanwhile, companies who, recognizing the inevitable, have already joined the rush toward ISO 9000, are enjoying the early benefits of universal acceptance. One corporation, Intertek, boasts in its advertising that its products are "ISO 9000 System Certified." A display ad published in magazines five years ago by Intertek proclaimed: *"With Intertek, You Won't Be Rejected on Seven Continents."*

In that ad, Intertek trumpets this message:

Intertek is one of the first U.S. companies with ISO 9000 certification traceable to an EC member state. That makes our certification *mark* immediately recognizable throughout the world. And more and more countries are enforcing these rigorous standards so our ISO 9000 certification will be increasingly essential for anyone who sells abroad. With the Intertek *mark*, your company name will have the respect and opportunities accorded to an

ISO 9000-certified organization. Without it, you could risk rejection on seven continents.

Surveillance Audits Required

Here is how the ISO 9000 program works, as explained in respected industrial publications:

> The ISO 9000 certification process uses a *third-party* system registration which means that an accredited or qualified assessor conducts an independent audit of an organization's quality system.
>
> Companies have to show evidence that their system is documented....Once certified, an operation undergoes *surveillance audits* twice a year to assure compliance of system changes and requirements.[5]

Donald W. Marquardt, writing in *Management Review* magazine, says that it can be costly to receive ISO 9000 certification: "The process can take as long as a year and cost $100,000 or more."[6]

But, if you don't have ISO 9000 approval, it can be even more costly. You eventually will be barred from selling your goods. Neil Maltra, of Volvo-General Motors and Heavy Trucks, reports that potential contractors without ISO 9000 who want to do business with his company are told to go elsewhere. He explains: "Potential suppliers who call are asked if they are in ISO 9000. If they say no, we say go and come back after you're qualified."[7]

Who's Behind ISO 9000?

Who runs Big Brother's ISO 9000 program? *Training* magazine, in a piece entitled, "What You Should Know About ISO 9000," says that, "ISO 9000 standards were developed during the 1980s by the *International Organization for Standardization (IOS)."*[8]

Quality magazine, another industrial source of information, explains that a group called the *National Accreditation Council for Certification Bodies (NACCB)*, headquartered in London, England, "is the official approving authority for third party registration boards in the United States."[9]

However, two American bodies, *The American Society of Quality Control (ASQC)*, Milwaukee, Wisconsin, and the *American National Standards Institute (ANSI)*, in New York city, are also being given authority to "accredit" registry board authorities throughout the U.S.A.[10]

Sorting it all out, we discover that just four, mysterious organizations, going by the odd acronyms *IOS, NACCB, ASQC,* and *ANSI,* will exercise virtually absolute and total control over this nation's entire product manufacturing and selling process! But, *who* are these organizations? *Who* set *them* up? *Who* controls them? *Who* gave them their authority?

The "Six-Sigma Quality" Program

To further extend control over the world's product markets, in addition to the ISO 9000 program, global industrial magnates have also established yet another so-called "quality" control system. In a *USA Today* business section article entitled, "U.S. Companies Push for Perfection," reporter John Hillkirk recently explained that the world's largest firms are now beginning to require something called *"six-sigma quality."*[11]

Many of the giant corporations involved in pushing the six-sigma program just happen to be active participants in the Council on Foreign Relations, the Trilateral Commission, and other globalist, New World Order organizations. Motorola, for example, has created an in-house Six-Sigma Quality Institute. Other corporations active in six-sigma quality are Eastman Kodak, L. L. Bean, IBM, Texas Instruments, Fuji, and Digital Equipment.

What exactly does the term "six-sigma" stand for?

U.S. companies push for perfection

By John Hillkirk
USA TODAY

A handful of U.S. companies are closing in on an unimaginable goal: Making products that have almost zero defects.

Motorola is now making several complicated products, including pagers and cellular telephones, that are 99.9996% defect-free. They contain less than 3.4 defects per million parts produced.

In statistical terms, that's known as the "six sigma" level of quality, and extremely few firms — including Japanese companies — are even close.

An amazing feat, true. But Motorola isn't stopping. Its new target, to be reached within six years, is 3.4 defects

per billion parts. "A lot of people say this is an insane level of improvement," says Mikel Harry, director of Motorola's Six Sigma Research Institute.

Others hitting top-quality standards:

► Eastman Kodak, the color film giant, has surpassed six-sigma quality in a couple of key product lines. Kodacolor film contains less than 1 defect per million parts produced.

► Catalog company L.L. Bean last spring shipped 500,000 packages without an error. But the company's error-free rate — 99.92% — still lags its manufacturing counterparts.

The typical U.S. product or service contains about 6,210 defects per million parts or errors per million transactions.

The IRS's tax advice telephone hot line has 140,000 errors per 1 million calls.

Why should companies aim so high?

► It saves money. Since 1987, Motorola's quality-improvement crusade has saved the company nearly $2.4 billion. That money would have been spent on factory rework, warranty repairs and inventory. Says Harry, "We're laughing all the way to the bank."

► Products are getting too complicated. Today's state-of-the-art computer memory chip contains 16 million microscopic transistors. Within 10 years, a chip will contain 1 billion devices. At that point, a single defect on a chip with a billion parts would ruin it.

In the same vein, Kodak says a

35mm film negative is made up of an almost infinite number of photographic elements. Eliminating every possible defect is a goal at Kodak as well as Japanese filmmakers Fuji and Konishiroku, maker of Koneca film.

With Motorola's help, several firms are striding toward similar improvements: IBM and Texas Instruments' Defense Systems and Electronics Group plan to achieve six-sigma quality throughout their product lines by 1994. Digital Equipment, six sigma by 1995.

"Several years ago, we didn't like to share anything," says Mike Cooney, quality chief at TI's defense/electronics arm. "But if we share, we're all going to get better faster."

Manufacturing companies support quality certification

POST NEWS SERVICES

More than three-fourths of Houston's manufacturing companies say they have achieved or will pursue certification under a series of international quality standards known as ISO 9000 because they believe this credential demonstrates their commitment to quality.

So says a new study by Grant Thornton, an accounting and management consulting firm with offices here.

In a mail survey of Houston manufacturers, Grant Thornton discovered that 82 percent of those that responded have taken or intend to take action regarding ISO 9000, which is required for many imports to foreign countries:

■ Twenty-seven percent of these manufacturing companies already have been certified under ISO 9000, a series of quality standards established by the Geneva-based International Organization for Standardization, which sets various measures and standards accepted worldwide.

■ Another 24 percent are going through the certification process now.

■ And 31 percent expect to become certified within the next two years.

Among the reasons Houston manufacturers cite for seeking certification under ISO 9000: ISO 9000 demonstrates a commitment to quality, 26 percent; major customers require or suggest certification, 24 percent; it will help compete internationally, 20 percent, and ISO 9000 provides a strategic advantage over non-certified competitors, 7 percent.

Michael R. Driessen, senior manager in the Houston office of Grant Thornton's Southwest area manufacturing and distribution practice, says certification under ISO 9000...

Greatland Corp. gains ISO 9000 certification

FROM STAFF REPORTS

Greatland Equipment & Services Corp. of Houston has become certified to ISO 9000 standards.

Bill Adams, Greatland's ISO 9000 program manager, said the effort took 18 months and involved every employee.

While ISO 9000 certification is an expensive, time-consuming process, Greatland founder Bill Gibbons said he "has no doubt it is the standard by which all companies will be judged, and only those who meet those criteria will enjoy continued domestic and international growth while other similar companies will now be playing catch-up and will be caught in the bottleneck created by the stampede for certification."

ation for intermediate petrochemical products.

"As worldwide market competition intensifies, more and more global corporations are demanding certified suppliers," said Ralph G. Coker, vice president and general manager of Coastal Refining and Marketing.

"Increasingly, our market has become worldwide, and the ISO 9000 certification confirms for our customers that Coastal Refining and Marketing processes and products are world-class."

Coastal's intermediate petrochemicals become ingredients for finished products ranging from nylon fiber to plastics.

The process — from raw materials to finished products — ... quality ...

These newspaper articles document that Big Brother control programs like ISO 9000 and Six-Sigma Quality are becoming mandatory for producers of goods in the U.S.A. and throughout the world.

This picture of a highway billboard illustrates the modern dilemma of mankind being controlled by bar code labels and marks. The Bible says that in the last days every person on earth will be forced to take a mark (Revelation 13).

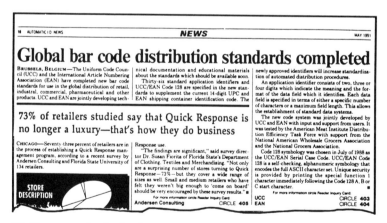

Uniform standards for bar codes have now been established for the whole world. Is this a precursor to the fulfillment of Bible prophecy?

Frankly, I don't know, but that fateful number *six* sure gets around these days, doesn't it?

Global Bar Code Adopted

Another control device in steady use throughout the world is the *bar code*. We see its ubiquitous use everywhere today on our supermarket products and in inventory warehousing systems of major companies. But did you know that, once again, the Illuminati has set up international organizations to oversee the standardization and *universal adoption* of bar codes? In 1991, from Brussels, Belgium in Europe came word that two groups, the *Uniform Code Council (UCC)* and the *International Article Numbering Association (EAN)*, had completed new bar code standards for use in the *global distribution* of retail, industrial, commercial, pharmaceutical, and other products.

Previously, every nation set its own standards for laser bar coding. But increasingly, all commercial outlets throughout the planet will be adopting the *global* numbering and coding system.

The World Trade Organization

The newly established *World Trade Organization (WTO)*, created by the Congress under the GATT bill, will tighten further the screws of ISO 9000, sigma-six, and the universal bar code system. In effect, we are moving fast into a dark era in which no man can buy or sell unless he has the mark, or the name, or the number of the Beast. Bible prophecy is coming to pass in a spectacular way.

Combined with the *Universal Biometrics Card* and the global system of human control under *Project L.U.C.I.D.*, ISO 9000 provides the coming World Government with a means of comprehensive control. Everything we own and have—even the privacy of our bodies—shall belong to the Beast.

SEVEN

Blood Money: Corporate Profiteering and the Making of Human Cyberslaves

Are we rapidly nearing the stage of total human slavery in the Technetronics Age? As I have exposed in *Circle of Intrigue* and other books, the men who comprise the inner circle of the Illuminati have a global plan. In implementing this plan, they appear to have the full cooperation of the planet's largest and most powerful high tech corporations. The world's premier telecommunications combine, of course, is that giant of giants, AT&T. AT&T will certainly play a significant part in the Information Superhighway now being created to support *Project L.U.C.I.D.*

Recently, it was announced that AT&T is splitting into three separate companies. One of the three—the company formerly known as Bell Laboratories—has been freshly renamed *Lucent Technologies*.

But, does AT&T's new baby have horns? Does the name *Lucent* have any link to the name *Lucifer?* Could it be that, as one writer has suggested, *Lucent* stands for *Lucifer's Enterprise?*

In the Bible, Lucifer is bequeathed the title, the "son of the morning." He is said to often come disguised as an "angel of light." He was anciently worshipped by pagans as "the Sun God, the Illumined One, the God of Light."

Modern-day New Age and Freemasonry groups continue this ancient glorification of Lucifer. One prominent New Age organization is the *Lucis Trust*. Its late founder, Alice Bailey, hailed the horned one as "bringer of light," the "shining one." He is, she trumpeted, the "Illuminator" of mankind.

Since Bailey's globalist occult group, the Lucis Trust, reveres Lucifer as the Illuminator of mankind and also promotes Freemasonry, with its Egyptian religion, I believe the true meaning of the name *Lucis* is *Lucifer plus Isis* (Isis was the Egyptian Mother Goddess). Thus, Luc + is = Lucis.

That Lucis is a combination word meaning *Luci*fer plus *Is*is is borne out by the fact that the Lucis Trust was first incorporated in 1922 as *Lucifer Publishing!*

Lucent Means "Glowing With Light"

Now, read carefully the article (see next page) published in *USA Today*, February 6, 1996, entitled, "AT&T Names the Baby: Lucent." Note especially AT&T's possibly revealing statement that the name for its spin-off corporation, *Lucent*, means "glowing with light."

The logo for the powerful new corporation is a rough-edged, red-colored *circle*. My latest book exposing the Illuminati, *Circle of Intrigue*, sheds light on the true and concealed meaning of the fiery, serpentine circle. Among the sources quoted in my book is Hislop's classic treatise, *The Two Babylons*. Hislop wrote: "In ancient Babylon, the King...a type of Antichrist...was acclaimed to be the Sun-god...the *Illuminator* of the material world...the *enlightener* of the souls of men."[1]

To occultists, the circle represents their satanic deity, the great and fearsome Solar Serpent. The fiery, red sun, or circle, is his image. Scriptures reveal him as the "great *red* dragon" and his global system as the scarlet (*red*-colored) beast (Revelation 12:3 and 17:3-5). How interesting that the logo for Lucent Technologies is a *red* circle.

Just as intriguing, in the *USA Today* article we read:

AT&T names the baby: Lucent

By Melanie Wells
USA TODAY

The company without a name finally got one.

AT&T will call the equipment company being created in the three-way split of the telecommunications giant Lucent Technologies.

Lucent? The name means glowing with light, or clear — even though it has little to do with what the company sells — telephone equipment.

AT&T named the company Monday in a Securities and Exchange Commission filing. It plans to offer Lucent shares in an initial public offering this spring.

AT&T hopes the name and logo — a simple, red circle — will illuminate awareness.

"There are a lot of new names in particular markets that are hitting right now; they'll have to buy their way in," says telecommunications analyst Jeffrey Kagan.

Industry experts say more than $100 million in advertising and marketing dollars will be spent to support the brand awareness push. Ads from agency McCann-Erickson will begin airing after Lucent's IPO.

Lucent was one of 700 names suggested by company employees and identity consultant Landor Associates. Among other contenders: American Bell Labs and AGB — short for telephone creator Alexander Graham Bell.

There's no consensus among brand experts, however. "My only doubt is it's a soft name; you want to look for it on supermarket shelves among the soaps," says Alan Brew, corporate identity specialist at Addison, Seefeld and Brew.

Says New England Consulting Group's Gary Stibel: "Initially, most people will think it sounds cute and not very good, but from a marketing standpoint it has potential."

▶ Lucent IPO, 6B

USA Today reported that Lucent was AT&T's choice of name for its baby Bell spin-off. Some are worried the baby has horns!

PUBLISHED FOR THE R&D COMMUNITY OF LUCENT TECHNOLOGIES

Bell Labs News

FEBRUARY 1996

Lucent Technologies Marks a New Beginning

BY LOREN TALLEY

Murray Hill, N.J. — The fresh white flag with the bold red logo flies in stark contrast to the sign in front of the building that says to all who drive past, "AT&T Bell Laboratories." But that sign and others like it will soon be altered to reflect a new dominion for Bell Labs.

The unveiling of Lucent Technologies on Feb. 5 signaled the end to an era at AT&T, and the dawn of a new industry age. Employees from around the globe celebrated the announcement of Lucent Technologies in an all-employee broadcast televised from Murray Hill — now the headquarters for the new company. The company also announced seven members of the new entity's board of directors, and filed with the Securities Exchange Commission that day for a planned offering of shares in the new entity.

"This marks a new chapter in the evolution of our company," said chairman and CEO Henry Schacht in his all-employee address. "When you bear one of the best known names in communications, selecting a new name takes on even more significance."

The name was whittled down from a list of 700 possible titles. As part of the naming process, the company conducted interviews and focus groups with employees

properties important in our processes. That is how people will distinguish us in the marketplace."

Schacht opened the broadcast on the morning of Feb. 5 by introducing the leadership team for Lucent Technologies. He thanked them for working to launch the new company, and reflected on the fact that 1995 was a challenging year as employees tried to serve their customers while dealing with AT&T's restructuring. "The past few months have been a tumultuous time, right up to the wee hours of last night [Feb. 4]."

Before the name was revealed, employees watched a video that poked fun at the previous anonymity of the new company. As tension mounted around the world, president and chief operating officer, Rich McGinn asked, "What will our future

be? What's in a name?" He went on to list the attributes to be embraced by the company's new identity. "We want to keep the best characteristics of the past, while adding new ones for our future." In its 127-year-old tradition the company has been known for its reliability, excellent service and integrity, and strong knowledge base, said McGinn. He also listed desirable images the company would strive for: speed, energy, flexibility, industry and customer focus, as well as innovation.

The auditorium burst into applause as the long-awaited name of Lucent Technologies was finally exposed. Immediately after, in an attempt to get people more acquainted with the company's new identity, McGinn asked each member of the audience to turn to and shake hands

with his neighbor and say, "Hi, I'm with Lucent Technologies." It was awkward at first, but people smiled as they formed the word, "Lucent" again and again. In addition, McGinn handed out gift-wrapped boxes of personalized business cards to a few specially chosen members of the audience.

McGinn readily acknowledged that people would have mixed emotions as they walked back to their offices that day, bringing the spirit of AT&T with them. But that spirit would only help the company succeed in going forward, he said. "With a new name, we have an opportunity to define ourselves," said McGinn. "You now own the new name. You *are* that name. And it's up to us to make it a wonderful name around the world." ■

Lucent Technologies
Bell Labs Innovations

"AT&T hopes the name and logo—a simple red circle—will *illuminate* awareness."

A Coincidence?

Perhaps AT&T's unfortunate choice of name (*Lucent* = *Lucifer*?) for its new, baby Bell spin-off, is a coincidence. Without definitive proof we cannot, with certainty, attribute evil intent. It could be that the eyebrow-raising and occult-infused language and terminology used by AT&T and quoted in the *USA Today* article—phrases like "illuminate awareness" and "glowing with light"—are incidental. But combined with AT&T's choice for a logo of the fiery-red circle so prevalent and prominent in pagan and other dark cultures, these things do, indeed, arouse inquiry and suspicion.

As if to emphasize this point, just days before I received the *USA Today* announcement, Living Truth Ministries received a phone call from an AT&T manager who is a Christian. He expressed horror that his company had done such a thing. Rejecting AT&T's assertion otherwise, this man flatly stated: "Many company employees suspect a Luciferian meaning to the chosen name, Lucent."

The caller also emphasized his belief in a connection between the curious circle logo adopted for Lucent Technologies and the occultic goals of the Illuminati as revealed in my book, *Circle of Intrigue.*

Writing in his excellent publication, *Midnight Messenger,* Christian researcher Des Griffin, author of *Fourth Reich of the Rich, Descent Into Slavery,* and other books, recently expressed his profound concern about AT&T's telling choice of name and logo for what was once the corporation's proud, Bell Labs division. He especially noted the veiled meaning of the symbology:

> Those familiar with the occult and New Age symbology understand what underlines all this. The leaders conceal their intentions in a multi-tiered code, and the higher up

one is in degree and study, the more understanding they have of the actual message being conveyed by the symbols.

One meaning of the red ring is the invincible sun (which, for years, has been exposed in the red "O" in Mobil). The sun is believed to be the giver and sustainer of all life. By those in the know, the light from that sun is understood—in its deep meaning—to represent Lucifer. The name Lucifer signifies light in Latin, as does the word "Lucent."

A further refining of this doctrine, which has been concealed from the public until now, is that the light means knowledge. As believed by the Ancients, those who possess knowledge are superior to others, and therefore worthy and duty-bound to use it to dominate and control those who do not possess it. These poor, unenlightened slobs would, of course, be grateful to have such benevolent characters (forcibly) guide them and tax them into poverty.

Lying deeper in this doctrine is the idea that people are their own gods, and that *human* knowledge and intellect alone are our savior and king. That so much should be exposed to the public demonstrates that we are at a critical *turning* point. Those who ascribe to this doctrine, and learn the symbols and conventions, are rewarded while others will, despite greater talent and aptitude, sometimes be passed over for promotion and recognition...[2]

An Empty Vessel to be Filled

"The greatest reality in the tangible world," says Des Griffin, "is what happens to our lives, families, and careers." Our families' lives, he continues, are deeply affected by our culture, and it is apparent that Lucent intends to impact culture. Griffin explains:

According to *Bell Labs News, Lucent* is "categorized by many as an *empty vessel*." *Bell Labs News* says, "We have decided on *Lucent* because we have a chance to fill this empty vessel with values, products, and the way we treat each other."

Those familiar with how AT&T has treated Christian employees in the past can see the foreboding future in these words of the CEO. To mention just one example, they have made it very difficult by firing or taking disciplinary action against any who do not openly approve of homosexuality.

The *empty vessel*—symbolic of the lives of most Americans in the 1990s—cannot be filled by more products, yet that is precisely what most people are being enticed to seek after; and *Lucent* stands only to profit from this. Clearly, the *values* with which AT&T's Mr. Schacht wishes to fill this "empty vessel" are not the values followed by the followers of the God of the Bible and the Lord Jesus Christ.[3]

Lucid, Lucent, Inferno: Hellish Similarities?

It deserves mention that the name *Lucent* is remarkable in its similarity to *Lucid*, or *L.U.C.I.D.* The long-time manager who wrote to me with his concerns about the direction his company was taking with the new logo and name—as well as its New Age-oriented personnel policies—told me that he sincerely believes that the true, but disguised, meaning of Lucent is *Lucifer's Enterprises*; in other words, *Luc-ent.*

As if to provide impetus to this notion, within days of my AT&T friend's letter and materials, I also received in the mail, from a member of the faculty in the Department of English at the University of Rochester, New York, a report just released by Lucent Technologies touting its "network operating system and programming environment." The name for this new, Lucent product staggered my imagination: *Inferno*. Yes, *Inferno*.

What's more, the logo for this highly touted product, *Inferno*, is the name "Inferno," printed in fiery, brimstone-like, edged type, surrounded by bellowing smoke!

Then I looked at the top of Lucent's publicity release and discovered this quote, from Dante's classic work, *The Inferno*:

> Day was departing, and the darkening air
> Called all earths' creatures to their
> evening quiet
> While I alone was preparing as
> though for war...
>
> *The Inferno of Dante, Canto II*

Dante's enduring work, *The Inferno*, was a tale of hell and of Lucifer! Thus, I asked myself, "Is Lucent not announcing that its new, global-wide internet connection product is of hellish, Luciferian origins?"

An Electronic Tower of Babel?

It was Lucifer, the master of hell, who, through his human servant, Babylon's Nimrod, defied God and sought to create a New World Order by building a colossal Tower of Babel. Nimrod's mighty efforts were ruined, however, when God confounded the builders by causing them to babble incoherently in different languages. Chaos ensued. How spellbinding it was to also read, in Lucent's press release for *Inferno*, a promotional quote by Peter Bernstein, president of Infonautics Consulting, who praised Lucent's software product with these words: "*Inferno* is designed to take the chaos out of the electronic Tower of Babel."

I delved further into the *Inferno* materials and discovered the statement by Lucent that, "Inferno (internet/computer) applications are written in a new language called *Limbo* which was designed specifically for the *Inferno* software environment."

Limbo? Isn't that a word, like purgatory, meaning to be suspended in a lower compartment of hell, awaiting judgment or punishment?

I also discovered that the "communications protocols" designed into Lucent's *Inferno* software are called *styx*. Now, in pagan mythologies and religion, *styx* is a synonym for the fiery, brimstone underworld region where devils reside. In other words: *hell!*

A Dark Message?

"Lucent...Inferno...Limbo...Styx!" What strange and dark message, I asked, is this corporate giant trying to send?"

Subsequently, in Lucent Technologies' own publication, *Bell Labs News*, I came across a rather enlightening article about Lucent Technologies' new, computer networking software system. Here's a portion of that article, written by Lucent's Patrick Regan and entitled, "Inside Inferno:"

> Dante's *Divine Comedy*, the medieval poem that inspired the name of the Inferno network operating system, recounts a metaphysical journey that begins with a guided tour of Hell and ends with a vision of Paradise. The story of the Inferno project is more modest in its setting, theme, and cast of characters, but it is definitely a story that ends happily.
>
> Inferno sped from research concept to the announcement of a new business venture in just 13 months, its progress fueled by close collaboration between inventors and executives. Its public launch met with enthusiastically positive responses from industry analysts and journalists. At this juncture, before Inferno's performance in the marketplace becomes the big story, *Bell Labs News* can offer a look inside Inferno—the concept, the project, and the technology.

Lucent Technologies
Bell Labs Innovations

Day was departing, and the darkening air
Called all earth's creatures to their evening quiet
While I alone was preparing as though for war...

The Inferno of Dante, Canto II

What is Inferno?

Inferno(tm) is a new network operating system and programming environment to deliver content in a rich environment of heterogenous networks, clients and servers.

The Inferno system includes the Inferno kernel, the Limbo(tm) programming language, reference APIs that include interfaces for networking and graphics, network protocols, security and

This is Lucent Technologies' press release announcing its new, computer network operating system, Inferno. The press release explains that Inferno software is written in a communications language called Limbo, with protocols called Styx. Curiously, the words, Inferno, Limbo, and Styx are all synonyms for hell!

Interactivity: Interactive television (ITV) was the initial target market for the creation of Inferno. Interactions between researchers and people close to the business broadened the idea of what the market needed, what network software technology could deliver, and what the team would pursue.

Early in 1995, according to Dennis Ritchie, head of Systems Software Research, a small group met at Murray Hill, New Jersey prompted by Bell Labs President Dan Stanzione and Bob Martin, then group technical officer for Network Systems—to discuss how software researchers—in particular the *Plan 9 team*—could advise or assist developers working on interactive TV systems.

The focus soon shifted from consultation on ITV to the invention of a network operating system to enable interactive applications using any media, any kind of network, and many kinds of communication devices, including personal computers, TV set-top boxes, games players, smart phones, and portable devices such as personal digital assistants.[4]

In plain English, the *Inferno* network system is designed to enable TVs, radios, phones, and other electronic products to become interactive and tied in to the *L.U.C.I.D.* net! Moreover, *Inferno* will create *interactive* capability: Today, you watch and hear the TV set in your living room. But someday soon, from a remote location, someone will be watching and hearing you—through *your* TV set.

Big Brother, clearly, is hard at work here. And George Orwell's vision of *1984* is at hand.

Circle of the Serpent King

As explained in my book, *Circle of Intrigue,* the hardened occultists who guide the activities of the Illuminati honor their lord, Lucifer, as the fiery-red, phoenix Serpent who, symbolically, is represented as the *circle*. Shown here is the supreme logo of Helena Blavatsky's *Theosophy*, a 19th century Luciferian organization which, in turn, spawned the modern conspiratorial group known today as Lucis Trust (*Luci*fer + *Is*is = Lucis).

Look carefully at this Luciferian logo. Observe its crowned Serpent's circle. Inside this circle is a secondary, almost hidden, inner circle, with an enclosed, swastika emblem. This inner circle and its swastika represent the exclusive, ten man *inner circle* of the Illuminati. These are the Wise Men. They are unmasked in *Circle of Intrigue* as Lucifer's depraved masterminds—super rich elitists driven mad by their greedy, insatiable appetites for money, control, and power.

These men are prophetically described as the "ten horns" (see Revelation 13 and 17) who oversee today's massive, global conspiracy. Their goal: cataclysmically cleanse the earth and "illuminate the awareness" of the remaining, thinned-out population by the year A.D. 2000, the bright dawning of their New Millennium.

New Offices at 666 Fifth Avenue

I've noted that AT&T's Lucent Technologies also has adopted as its logo the fiery, red circle. We've analyzed the name *Lucent*, itself, and examined its hellishly named, innovative products. Is there an even stranger coincidence indicating this corporation's connection with the Beast, 666, and his globo-cop computer system, *L.U.C.I.D.?* Indeed, there is!

Crain's (formally, *Crain's New York Business*) is one of that city's most influential and respected business publications. It is eagerly read by New Yorkers and the Wall Street crowd. In its July 1-7 (1996) issue, on page one, we find this staggering bit of information, repeated here exactly as it was printed:

Lucent Looks For Space

Lucent Technologies, the $21 billion former equipment division of AT&T, is cruising Manhattan for space. The company has already signed a lease for 40,000 square feet at 666 Fifth Ave. at a rent estimated in the high $30s per square foot and is now looking at an additional 150,000 square feet at Financial Square in downtown Manhattan. Cushman & Wakefield represents Lucent. The landlords—Sumitomo Realty at 666 Fifth and Paramount Group at Financial Square—are acting on their own behalf.

What kind of mind-warping coincidence is this? Lucent Technologies, the company with the red, circle logo that gives us its amazing, new internet *Inferno* software, is moving into offices at *666 Fifth Avenue!* The number 666, we know from the book of *Revelation*, identifies the Beast. The number "five" (as in *Fifth*) is the number of the dead in occult and Masonic numerology. So, once again, I ask: Are all these things mere coincidences?...Or, is this all evidence that *Lucent Technologies* is, indeed, an Illuminati proprietary group?

A Brave New Technetronic World

Today, we have the Mark of the Beast identification system being constructed practically before our eyes. Meanwhile, under the watchful supervision of the Illuminati, all the world's military intelligence, spy, and police agencies are laboring furiously to invent ever more effective, electronic, high tech shackles. The intent of the controllers is to force us, as slaves, into a Brave New Technetronic World. Their projected target date is the year 2000.

Suddenly, the planet's premier telecommunications

company creates a research and development spin-off named Lucent Technologies. Will the innovative brains at the venerable company known historically as Bell Laboratories, but now dubbed Lucent, be active in carrying out Big Brother's unholy mission of technetronic control?

Will Lucent's world-class scientists and engineers be at the forefront in the development of advanced tools of human control which I have categorized as "black science?" Will Lucent Technologies assist in inventing the wiretap equipment, microchips, spy and surveillance systems, artificial intelligence, virtual reality, robotic controls, and other devices which shall usher in the final and ultimate Age of Technetronics? Will Lucent play a key role in instituting new, high tech equipment and methods which will make possible the grim, financial control system prophesied in God's Holy Bible?

It may well be that the men who now are the brains behind Lucent and the other corporations mentioned here have no conception of how their creative "children"—products like Lucent's *Inferno, Limbo,* etc.—fit in to the end-time scenario. Without definitive and irrefutable proof, I am not ready to label these men as willing and knowing agents of the Evil One. Still, Satan is more than capable of using even the most sincere of *unwitting* dupes and stooges to do his dirty work here on earth. Imagine the damage he can do with the products produced by the brilliant men who roam the halls and corridors of the world's premier high technology establishments and laboratories!

What some may envision as commercial breakthroughs intended to be man's *helpers* may, inevitably, turn out to be products which result in the *oppression* of man.

The Corporate Connection: Huge Profits to Be Made

My investigation into and comments regarding AT&T's Lucent Technologies is not intended to single out just one U.S.A. company or one multinational firm. Indeed, over the past few years the corporate world has gone crazy researching and developing advanced means of computer control. They do so primarily for profit—there are significant fortunes to be made in helping push Big Brother's stunning, new systems forward into effective operation.

Just consider, for example, what Ronald Kane, a vice president of Cubic Corporation's automatic revenue collection group, had to say recently about his company's innovative, high tech devices used in control systems. "If we had our way," said Kane, "we'd implant a chip behind everyone's ear in the maternity ward."[5]

According to *Popular Science* magazine, Mr. Kane's Cubic Corporation is one of many actively "pushing the frontier of smart cards—the money of the future."[6] Smart Cards, of course, are not mere pieces of plastic—they are tiny, portable computers. Smart Cards, *Popular Science's* Phil Patton observes, will very soon be so futuristic they will "be validated biomorphically by fingerprints or (eye iris) retinal readers." The cashless society of the year 2000, made possible by the Smart Card, may someday even be superseded, says Patton, "with a chip implanted under our skins..."[7]

The price of Cubic Corporation's stock has shot up like a rocket on the exchanges in recent years, a sure sign that knowledgeable insiders and savvy investors see the field of cyber-control products a booming area of high profitability. When Lucent Technologies stock was offered initially in April, 1996, shares quickly rose 13 percent in one day, setting a Wall Street record for first-day trading volume.[8]

But nothing—not even the sky-high Lucent shares—can match the stratospheric ascent of the shares of a small company named *Comparator*. Comparator is a new company marketing an advanced type of biometric, fingerprint identification device. In May of 1996, Nasdaq market records show that the stock shares of the tiny company known as Comparator rose an astounding *2,900 percent* in just three days!

What's more, this fantastic rise even came amidst reports that the financial condition of the company was abysmal![9]

While Comparator, Cubic, and Lucent have seen their shares zoom to cosmological heights, the three are by no means the only companies to have the mouths of investors and money managers salivating with greed. Such corporations as Fingermatrix, U.S. West, Scanpoint, Polaroid, Oracle, DataCard, Bloodhound Sensors, Identix, TRW, Harris, Gemplus, Microscan, Malco, Danyl, Cotag, Identicator, Trigon, Symbology, Fargo Electronics, Recognition Systems, and scores of others are prospering.

Big Brother, apparently, has scads of loose change, and he's more than willing to spread it around. The prophetic control system I identify as *Project L.U.C.I.D.* is being built—and fast.

To Devour the Whole Earth

What once was inconceivable has now entered the realm of possibility—even the *circle* of reality. Lucent Technologies and thousands of other high tech research corporations and centers are briskly pushing us—every last one of us— into that brutal and frightening era in which the final, rushing blows will be delivered to man by his controllers. They do so in the quest for profit, some not understanding that the money made may, someday soon, when Big Brother begins his purge and cleansing of society, become "blood money."

The Bible prophet, Daniel, was shown a vision of this very age—the Age of Technetronics, of human slavery. Daniel's vision foresaw four beast kingdoms that would rule the earth in historical succession. Now we are seeing and experiencing the momentous emergence of the last and final kingdom, or global authority, on planet earth— that of the Fourth Beast Kingdom.

Yes, the prophesied, last days Beast is slouching toward Jerusalem. He is, moreover, setting up his heinous and intrusive technological systems around the globe, filling up every nook and cranny with his high tech eyes and ears, and his bloody, electronic hands.

Very soon, the citizens of the U.S.A. and, indeed, the whole earth will begin to shake and quiver before the unstoppable onslaught of this unbridled, technological fury:

> Thus he said, The fourth beast shall be the fourth kingdom upon earth, which shall be diverse from all kingdoms, and shall devour the whole earth, and shall tread it down, and break it in pieces. (Daniel 7:23)

"Watch ye, therefore..."

Are you ready for the rapid-coming arrival of the Fourth Beast and his dark, technological marvels? Is your life in order? Are you trusting only in the Lamb of God for your protection and sustenance? Be alert, be sober, be vigilant, the prophetic scriptures warn: "Watch ye therefore: for ye know not when the master of the house cometh...Lest coming suddenly he find you sleeping" (Mark 13:35-36).

EIGHT

A Worldwide Project of the Illuminati

I s there a global-wide *conspiracy* to require every man, woman, and child to receive a personal number and a smart, microchip-integrated, I.D. card? Remember, in earlier chapters, I demonstrated and presented irrefutable evidence that the *L.U.C.I.D.* net, as designed, will encompass a *universal* police state. No one is to be allowed to escape its high tech handcuffs.

Most people are woefully and tragically ignorant of the world conspiracy of the elite, and of the hidden plan of the few who reign at the top echelon of the elite— whom I refer to as the *Illuminati*. But the late Professor Carroll Quigley of Georgetown University was not ignorant. He knew of this vast conspiracy to shackle the people of the world because he had access to their most secret records. Quigley was President Bill Clinton's political mentor and was recognized as such by then candidate Clinton during his 1992 nominating acceptance speech at New York City's Madison Square Garden. In his book, *Tragedy and Hope*, Quigley revealed that the aim of this monstrous conspiracy of the few is "nothing less than to create a World System of financial control in private hands able to dominate the political system of each country and the economy of the world as a whole."[1]

Regrettably, Professor Carroll Quigley identified with and approved of the aims of the Illuminati. The late Arnold Toynbee, Britain's famous, socialist historian of world history, also saw the conspiracy as a harbinger of good.

For civilization to evolve, he declared, all independent nations "ought to be deprived of their sovereignty and subordinated to the sovereignty of a global government."[2]

Global Government the Goal

The completion of *Project L.U.C.I.D.* will rapidly move America and the nations of the world into the arms of a global government, a cherished goal of world federalists such as Quigley and Toynbee. It will also fulfill George Orwell's vision of a frightening future, as depicted in his novel, *1984*. As Frenchman Jean-Marie Le Pen, head of France's anti-New World Order *National Front Party*, stated in a thoughtful interview recently, the real danger does not come from terrorists and ethnic hate groups, but from *globalists and internationalists* bent on creating a world system of human control:

> It is evident that the danger of a communist domination over the world has been replaced by a globalist and mercantile domination. This ideology aims at world government by a small financial oligarchy, backed by the United Nations and the various international enforcement agencies. The proponents of this new world domination consider the nations of the world as their principal enemies. It is their aim to weaken them and then destroy the nations. Once this is accomplished, then will come the reign of "Big Brother," described in (George) Orwell's *1984*...

Mr. Le Pen sounds a warning and a recommendation we should all heed:

> Let us not be mistaken about this: We are witnessing a veritable conspiracy to create a global power that would deprive the people of their national independence. I believe that the nation is still the best political framework to ensure the defense, the independence, the security, the

identity, the freedom and the prosperity of people.[3]

The *L.U.C.I.D.* net will cut across national boundaries. It will require a mandatory *Universal Biometrics Card*—and eventually an implanted biochip—for the citizens of France, the U.S.A., Britain, Germany, China, Brazil—every country on earth. With its 2,000 page memory, its ability to contain an entire dossier of private information, and its capacity to be used for individual purchases and financial transactions, the *universal I.D.* and its link with a *global computer network* will inevitably mean the bypassing and ruination of the world's ages-old, nation-state system. God's Word says He will "judge the nations." But the Illuminati are defiant, and thus, *the Tower of Babel is being reconstructed.*

This, in fact, is the hidden agenda of the global conspirators. In his book, *Inside the New Age Nightmare*, Randall Baer, a former, top New Age leader and author who became a born again Christian and went on to expose this massive, elitist conspiracy for world hegemony, alluded to this when he wrote:

This agenda is nothing less than the complete revolutionizing of the very foundations of not only America but the entire world. Such a plan calls for the total restructuring of planetary civilization into an enlightened One World Federation in which national boundaries and sovereignty are secondary, and "planetary citizenship" in the "global village" is the order of the day. This (conspiracy) offers a world in desperate need a grand solution to profound global problems. Apparent world peace and unprecedented opportunities...are to be unveiled. Herein lies the Antichrist's last temptation, offered to all the world.[4]

Ancient Roots of the Conspiracy

But, how could a global conspiracy of immense, *behemoth* proportions gain such incredible headway in such a short span of time? After all, the computer revolution can be traced back only to the last few decades. The answer is that the conspiracy has its roots in very *ancient* occultism. The conspirators have strived for untold centuries to usher in a One World Order, but they have been stymied in their efforts to complete their awful agenda.

Now, however, the missing quotient has been found—the ingredient that shall, at long last, culminate and crown their efforts with success. The *computer*, and more specifically, the *global networking of computers*, is that powerful, but once missing, quotient. With the computer net and its linked sensors has come the ability to establish total control and enslavement of the world's populations.

Few people recognize that mankind has, for centuries, been guided toward an occult destiny by use of what 33° Masonic scholar Manly P. Hall described as a *Universal Motion*. In his book, *The Secret Destiny of America*, Hall points to the reality of the Illuminati—"enlightened human beings united in...an Order of the Quest." These higher consciousness, enlightened humans, Hall suggests, are driving the world ever deeper toward globalization and centralized power. Yet, he notes, "the great masses of people still live along without any knowledge whatever that they are part of a *Universal Motion*."[5]

A Universal Motion? Is that what *Project L.U.C.I.D.* is all about? Are peoples everywhere being shepherded into a dark and solitary, consolidated, cyberworld concentration camp? Are men, women, and children being herded—through this Universal Motion—into locked, *silicon cages*, watched over by biological sensors and computerized sentries?

Can this attempt to push us into our silicon cages by the mechanism of a *Universal Motion* be verified and proven? Does documentation and evidence exist?

The answer is *yes*. It is easily demonstrated that, across the globe, governments everywhere are involved *simultaneously* and with great, energetic maneuvering, in herding humanity into the *L.U.C.I.D.* cauldron. Take, for example, the requirement for the biometrics I.D. card.

Beginning in 1993, dozens of governments, in concert, initiated national legislation and bureaucratic programs to cram I.D. cards down the throats of their combined citizenries:

The Netherlands: A new law was passed requiring citizens to carry I.D. cards on their persons at all times. The data integrated into the card contains the individual's tax file number, name, address, and nationality. Persons not able to produce an I.D. card are already being arrested and jailed.[6]

Singapore: A mandatory program to register all citizens and issue them high tech, laser-engraved I.D. cards was completed in 1994. According to Sydney, Australia's *Sunday Mag,* "The new I.D. will enable the government to keep electronic tabs" on citizens. The publication said that, "The credit card-sized 'smart' cards have photographs, thumb prints, personal details, and machine-readable bar codes that keep the owner's number and personal data ready for official inspection."[7]

Japan: In the *Japan Times* newspaper in 1996 we read: "Though there is fierce resistance in the United States to issuing government I.D. numbers to everyone, in Japan a similar plan is being pursued successfully by the Japanese government. Bills will be introduced in the Diet (legislature) in 1997 with plans to give everyone their own number by 1999. The number will be used to identify everyone for taxes, voting, passport control, and many other functions."[8]

Canada: From the *London Free Press,* Ottawa, Canada, we read: "Not everyone is keen on Premier Mike Harris' idea of a national identity card...The new conservative premier said that Ontario might fingerprint cards to be used for health care, drivers licenses, and welfare. He suggested Ottawa use the same number to track unemployment insurance and other benefits."[9]

Canada is fast becoming a high tech police state and is joining hands with its southerly neighbor, the U.S.A., in this globalist venture. In *Biometrics Today* magazine, it was reported that Canada and the United States are working together to introduce a system of optical memory cards with fingerprint identification and voice recognition features. Eventually, all travelers crossing the U.S./Canada border will be required to have the "compass" I.D. card.[10]

Australia: According to the *Sydney Morning Herald,* I.D. cards are being made mandatory for all aussies. Meanwhile, Australia's political circles are teeming with more and more sophisticated plans for electronic control of the masses.[11] In the Australian newspaper, *Melbourne Age,* came this recent report: "Australians could soon be wearing wristbands carrying their electronic signature, age, bank account details, and other information needed to conduct electronic transactions...Steve Orlawski, a special advisor to the federal Attorney-General's department, sees the idea of a wristband merely as a more convenient form of the smart cards being developed...He says you could have a tax file number, medical card number, bank account number, any extent of information on the card."[12]

If the electronic wristband is adopted, will it become simply a precursor to the eventual biochip implant, either in the forehead or the right hand?

Thailand: All Thai citizens have, in recent years, been issued I.D. cards. Information on the cards is linked in to a Control Data computer network, with connections to tax departments and criminal law enforcement authorities. *Time* magazine reported on the Big Brother aspects of the Thai I.D. card network:

> As a newcomer to the world of computers, the government of Thailand was surprised and flattered last summer when it won a prize for being a "hero of the information age" from the Smithsonian Institution and *Computerworld* magazine...Technocrats may admire systems like Bangkok's, which by 2006 will have stored vital data on 65 million Thais in a single, integrated computer network. But civil libertarians are appalled.
>
> Simon Davies, an Australian expert on such technology for the watchdog group Privacy International, says

Bangkok's prizewinning program is, potentially, "one of the most repressive surveillance systems the world has ever seen."

Thailand's population database system—the largest of its kind—has become a symbol for an alarming trend....
Some of (the) biggest computer firms have begun selling to Third World governments systems that are far more invasive than any permitted back home. In some cases, though not necessarily Thailand's, computers with vast potential for misuse are being sold to governments...

Behind Thailand's new I.D. cards are a $50 million computer system and sophisticated software that could enable a Big Brother government to create a dossier quickly that would tell it just about anything it wanted to know about anybody.[13]

The same *Time* article reported that U.S. technology is now being used in South Africa and Israel to control people whom the government suspects as being potentially troublesome.

Time also reported that, "Guatemala, where death squads have been linked to hundreds of extrajudicial executions and disappearances, purchased computer surveillance software from Israel in the early 1980s."[14]

Still, said the magazine, high tech corporations are looking to make sizeable profits. "Taiwan is expected to award contracts worth $270 million for its own residential-information system. Among the bidders: Unisys, Digital Equipment Corp., NEC, and ICL."[15]

Russia: From the days of Lenin and Stalin, Russia has had a national (or Soviet-wide) identification system for its enslaved peoples. But today, with the invention of computers and the global internet, the Kremlin's police and spy masters are ecstatic. They're working extremely close on a daily basis with their United States counterparts, to integrate Russia and its nearby, so-called independent, neighboring republics into the universal system.

The FBI has opened an office in Moscow and has top agents assigned there now. This is the first time ever that this has occurred. (Evidently, director Louis Freeh forgot that the FBI is a *federal*, not a *global* police agency.)

"America's FBI has kindly agreed to render us assistance," said Sergei Stepashin, head of Russia's counterintelligence. The FBI is now training Russian policemen at its FBI Academy in Quantico, Virginia. The CIA, meanwhile, is hosting Russian KGB operatives at the CIA's Langley, Virginia, headquarters complex, while the Department of Defense has brought tens of thousands of Russian, special forces commandos to the United States for "anti-terrorist" training. The Russian soldiers have been photographed at Fort Drum, New York; Ft. Hood, Texas; Fort Polk, Louisiana; and elsewhere.[16]

In a visit to the capital city of Slavakia, a former, Soviet East European nation, FBI Director Freeh praised East-West cooperation in law enforcement. "The world is getting smaller, and the need for police to work together is becoming more important," Freeh claimed. Freeh pointed to the continuing problem of "hate groups" as an example of why global cooperation is now necessary.[17]

Traveling with Freeh on a ten day trip to Eastern European countries was the head of America's Drug Enforcement Agency (DEA), the Secret Service Director, and the Assistant Treasury Secretary.[18]

Great Britain: In 1994, evidently acting on orders from the Illuminati, Prime Minister John Major's government suddenly began a nation-wide propaganda campaign to seduce the British population to accept a computerized I.D. card network. In an interview in London's *The Daily Telegraph*, the Prime Minister suggested that the proposed system could play a part in "fighting crime." Besides, Major insisted, an I.D. card network will enjoy "broad public support."[19]

Shortly afterwards, a cabinet official announced that Englanders would be issued a "smart I.D. card by the year 2000." As *The Guardian* newspaper reported: "A design for Britain's first government-issued, personal identity smart card has been shown to the cabinet...the card could replace the driving license, passport, pension book, and medical card of every person...and will use biometrics and passwords."[20]

However, apparently the government's rosy plans for a mandatory I.D. card system did not enjoy the "broad public support" of which the Prime Minister had boasted. Instead, according to London's *The Daily Mail*, the British people caused a considerable ruckus—"they revolted," the newspaper reported. Fearing the public backlash, government ministers quickly announced that the I.D. card system would be "voluntary," not compulsory. (But once the government has its foot in the door, who really believes this fiction about a "voluntary" I.D. card system?)[21]

France: The country of France, which has suffered foreign invasions during two world wars this century, regrettably, is under assault once again. This time, it's a silent invasion by the cunning organizers of the global *L.U.C.I.D.* net. According to Dr. Jean-Paul Creusat and Anthony Halaris, designers of *L.U.C.I.D. net*, France's *Interpol*, an intergovernmental police agency, has been chosen to "demonstrate the feasibility and practicality of *L.U.C.I.D.* System to the criminal justice system."[22]

If anyone reading this doubts that conspiratorial spade work to implement *Project L.U.C.I.D.* has been accomplished on all the globe's seven continents, just read what Creusat and Halaris say about Interpol's role in executing the *L.U.C.I.D.* system:

> INTERPOL was a non-governmental organization under the name of International Criminal Police Commission, founded in September 1923 in Vienna, Austria. The organization was reconstituted and transferred its headquarters from Vienna to Paris in 1946. The present name, ICPO-INTERPOL, was adopted in 1977 after the latest amended constitution in Stockholm, Sweden. Presently, INTERPOL is acting as an inter-governmental organization and its headquarters are located in Lyon, France. The Secretary General is Mr. Raymond E. Kendall.

The Daily Telegraph

NEWSPAPER OF THE YEAR

NO 42,351   WEDNESDAY, JUNE 8, 1994

Major backs ID cards to fight crime

● Dividend controls ruled out
● Anti-IRA supremo rejected

INTERVIEW

By George Jones
Political Editor

THE FEASIBILITY of introducing a national identity card that could store a range of instantly accessible information about the holder on a magnetic strip is being examined by the Government, the Prime Minister disclosed in an interview with *The Daily Telegraph* yesterday.

Mr Major believes that such a card cou... fighting crim... ...oad...

...which would contain information including National Insurance records. It could also double as a driving licence. Home Office figures

values despite evidence of economic recovery.

Mr Major is understood to have been concerned by the apparent alarm in the City that the Government was hostile to dividend payments and he went out of his way yesterday to provide reassurance that the Treasury was not planning new controls.

Business Post

Vol XLIX No 245   BANGKOK THURSDAY SEPTEMBER 2 1994   2A   SECTION TWO

Bangkok Post Friday September 2, 1994

Drivers licenses with computer chip

The National Police Agency is considering introduction of IC "smart card" drivers licenses that could be used as identity cards or even to start a car.

The data storage capability of cards with integrated circuits, agency officials said, could make it possible to imbed in the cards such essential identity information as name, address, emergency notification information, and records of traffic violations.

The information can be read by a portable device that will be carried by traffic police. It added the licenses will be about the same size as credit cards and the new driving licenses that were introduced in May.

The cards will help facilitate the issuance of traffic violation tickets by giving police easy access to drivers' records and enabling police to input violations quickly. Police will also be ...le to...

Is it by coincidence that, across the globe, national political leaders and national law enforcement agencies suddenly "decided" to issue Smart I.D. Cards to their combined citizenries?

Technology

Peddling Big Brother

Foreign governments are snapping up surveillance systems that are produced—but proscribed—in the West

By PHILIP ELMER-DEWITT WASHINGTON

As a newcomer to the world of computers, the government of Thailand was surprised and flattered last summer when it won a prize for being a "hero of the information age" from the Smithsonian Institution and *Computerworld* magazine. The award, which focused world attention on the Interior Ministry's efforts to computerize the country's social services, proved to be a mixed blessing. Technocrats may admire systems like Bangkok's, which by 2006 will have stored vital data on 65 million

long histories of human-rights violations.

At first glance the Thai system, which is being considered for possible adoption by Indonesia and the Philippines, seems harmless enough. Every citizen over age 15 will be required to carry a card bearing a color photo, various pertinent facts (name, address and so on) and an identification number. Most Thais are happy to get their IDs, which distinguish citizens from noncitizens (including a large population of refugees) and simplify all sorts of bureaucratic transactions, from receiving healthcare benefits to enrolling a child in school.

WITH THIS CARD, THE THAI GOVERNMENT CAN OBTAIN:

Her name and picture
Her fingerprints
Her height
Her home address
Her parents' names
Her children's names
Her marital status
Her education
Her occupation and income
Her nationality and religion
Her family history
and if the links are made
Her tax return
Her criminal record (if any)

Time magazine (June 24, 1991)

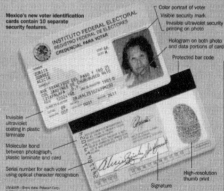

USN&WR (August 15, 1994)

Eliminating the crazy rat

Mexicans have developed a rich vocabulary for the methods used by mapaches (electoral engineers) to ensure that the institutional Revolutionary Party always wins. The *cambio de pañal* (diaper change) means changing the voter list at the polling place. The *ratón loco* (crazy rat) means shuffling voter lists and forcing voters to run around to find where they are listed. The *carrusel* means taking loyal voters to vote at different places. The *taco* means stuffing a roll of ballots in the box.

Now the PRI government is using high technology to help clean up this month's elections. The centerpiece of reform is a 2-by-3-inch piece of plastic, the largest voter photo identification program in history. Using a database of voters developed by IBM, Booz-Allen & Hamilton and Oracle, a California software company, the Mexican subsidiary of Polaroid produced the cards; the government has spent $730 million to deliver them to 45.7 million voters.

Mexico's new voter identification cards contain 10 separate security features.

Color portrait of voter
Visible security mark
Invisible ultraviolet security printing on photo
Hologram on both photo and data portions of card
Protected bar code
High-resolution thumb print
Signature
Serial number for each voter using optical character recognition
Molecular bond between photograph, plastic laminate and card
Invisible ultraviolet coating in plastic laminate

From Thailand to Mexico, governments have suddenly begun to issue computer-linked I.D. cards. Who's behind this global campaign?

The ICPO-INTERPOL plays a key role as the Central Command for the joint efforts of the national law enforcement agencies of its 174 Member Countries official police bodies. The work of ICPO-INTERPOL is financed by contributions from its member countries. The commitment is to ensure and promote widest possible mutual assistance between all police authorities within the limits of laws existing in 174 countries and in the spirit of the (United Nations) Universal Declaration of Human Rights. Today's task is to establish and develop special projects likely to contribute effectively to prevention and suppression of international crimes. These special projects components are as follows:

- the establishment of a structured and coordinated system for collecting and processing information;

- the use of this system to provide national services with investigative leads and to enhance cooperation in connection with investigations; and

- technical studies and proposals to enable national services to adapt their tactics and strategies.[23]

Creusat and Halaris go on to say:

The NCB-INTERPOL provides an essential communication link between a member country police community and counterparts in the foreign member countries. The United States participation in INTERPOL began in 1938 by congressional authorization, designating the Attorney General as the official representative to the organization. INTERPOL operations were interrupted during World War II, but resumed in 1947. The Attorney General officially designated the Secretary of the Treasury as the US representative to INTERPOL in 1958, and the US National Central Bureau was established within the Treasury. This Memorandum of Understanding designates the Attorney General as the permanent representative to INTERPOL and the Secretary of the Treasury as the alternate representative.

The USNCB operates through cooperative efforts with federal, state and local law enforcement agencies. Programs and initiatives, such as the State Liaison Program and the Canadian Interface Project, broaden the scope of investigative resources to include the international community, thus forming an integral part in efforts to confront the problem of international crime. Under the State Liaison Program, states establish an office within their own law enforcement community to serve as liaison to USNCB. International leads developed in criminal investigations being conducted by a state or local entity can be pursued through their Liaison Office, and criminal investigative requests from abroad are funneled through the relevant state liaison office for action by the appropriate state or local agency. All 50 states now participate in the liaison program, which is coordinated by a representative from State Police. USNCB has two sub-bureaus which serve to more effectively address the law enforcement needs of US territories. The sub-bureaus are located in San-Juan, Puerto Rico; and Pago Pago, American Samoa.[24]

The Hidden Role of the National Security Agency

We discover, then, that according to L.U.C.I.D.'s organizers, the Paris, France-based global cop agency known as Interpol "plays a key role as the Central Command for the joint efforts of the national law enforcement agencies of its 174 Member Countries' official police bodies."[25]

The United States, through the Departments of Treasury and Justice, coordinates with Interpol in pursuing its globo-cop mission.

I believe, however, that it is the National Security Agency (NSA) which is funding and orchestrating this whole charade. Interpol, I am convinced, is simply an organizing tool of the globalists. This is true also of another newly established, super intelligence agency called *Europol*.[26] But while Interpol may serve temporarily as the "Central Command," the Illuminati plot out their agenda and issue commands to a worldwide legion of servants via their Goliath-sized apparatus known as the *National Security Agency*, located at Fort Meade, Maryland.

The United States is, in fact, the one nation with the technological moxie, know-how, and wealth needed to establish the Antichrist's all seeing eye apparatus. We are the land that invented the electrical grid, the computer, the microchip, the laser, and the internet. Now, there's *L.U.C.I.D.* to add to the list.

United States: While the peoples of every nation on earth, thanks to the world conspiracy, are being agitated into *L.U.C.I.D.* as part of a "Universal Motion," the domination of the pivotal U.S.A. is key to the Illuminati's plan of an escape-proof, universal, *Project L.U.C.I.D.* control system. That's why everyone, from U.S. Senator Kay Bailey Hutchison (R.-TX) to U.S. Senator Diane Feinstein (D.-CA), has been clamoring to obey their marching orders, introducing legislation to require a *national* I.D. card linked into a *global* computer network. In other words, controlled politicians on both ends of the spectrum—Republican and Democrat (and in-between!) are vigorously stumping for a *L.U.C.I.D.* system.

In 1996, Texas Senator Hutchison introduced *Senate Bill 999* (999 reversed equals 666!) to mandate federal-issued I.D. cards. Her liberal counterpart, Senator Feinstein, was everywhere on Capitol Hill just the year before, in 1995, giving speeches and issuing press releases calling for the implementation of what can only be described as the *Beast 666 Universal Human Control System*.

In the influential, Washington, D.C. political newspaper *Roll Call*, Feinstein was quoted as urging that the biometrics, retina scan I.D. card be hurried into service, with all "the databases needed to support it."[27]

The Senator, who only a few years before, in 1992, bashed political commentator Patrick Buchanan and other conservatives for attempting to put a lid on illegal immigration, suddenly, in 1995, did a dramatic spin-about. She explained that the I.D. Big Brother network was a desperate necessity; only it, she urgently explained, can "solve the illegal immigration crisis!" When asked, shouldn't we study this issue further?, Feinstein haughtily replied, "No, we've got to do it now, and quick," adding:

> Shouldn't we simply press forward with a single integrated system now, require everyone to obtain the new documents within a reasonable phase-in period, and subject that document (I.D. card) to annual renewals...?[28]

In the *Roll Call* interview, Senator Feinstein had it all down pat. She had been well-briefed. The new I.D. card, as she detailed it, would be advanced high tech, "with a microchip, magnetic bar code, voice print, retina pattern, digitally coded fingerprint, and digitized photo."[29]

Having Pity on Hitler and Stalin

Compared to the proposals put forward by Hutchison, Feinstein, and so many other establishment politicians, perhaps we should have pity for poor old Uncle Adolf and Uncle Josef. After all, Adolf Hitler had to labor tirelessly, locating Jews and Christian enemies with old-fashioned identification methods—like tattoos and papers. And Josef Stalin's Communist commissars were handicapped in that they kept notoriously unreliable records of their Soviet gulag victims.

The mind boggles to imagine what extraordinary powers of control tomorrow's tyrants shall wield, once the *Project L.U.C.I.D.* system is firmly entrenched. If they were alive on earth, how envious the bloody duo, Hitler and Stalin, would be, gazing at all the technological wizardry available to today's modern version of their infamous jackbooted thugs.

Perhaps FBI Director Louis Freeh said it best shortly

after his appointment to the Federal Bureau of Investigation in 1993. Referring to the incredible array of computerized control and battle gadgetry available to federal law enforcement, Freeh, stressing cooperation and teamwork between his own FBI and the other alphabet police agencies, sardonically remarked, *"Let's share our toys."*

NINE

Silicon Octopus: Men Trapped Inside Electronic Cages

There is a plan to bring America into a New World Order," writes Dwight Kinman in his insight-filled book, *The World's Last Dictator*. In reality, Kinman says, "The New World Order is the secret code phrase for a one world government."[1]

This plan, Kinman adds, "is gathering momentum and accelerating with the speed of a runaway freight train:"[2]

> Behind this plan are powerful, global, megaforces that are on an inexorable, relentless drive to establish, on planet earth, a super world government by the year A.D. 2000. They believe they have it almost within their grasp, and they are about to make a dash to the finish line.[3]

I am convinced by a mountain of evidence that Dwight Kinman is correct. The hidden plan for a super world government *is* in its final stages of completion. But, if so, why haven't the media reported it? Why are the American people so abominably ignorant and so painfully oblivious to what is happening? Why are they not more alarmed about the loss of personal privacy and freedom that is resulting from the continuing growth of Big Brother's technological chains?

It is not only the *L.U.C.I.D.* net, its remote sensors, its

Universal Biometrics Card, and its future implantable biochip we are talking about. As invasive as this system is, Big Brother has many more tools in the realm of Black Science. In his eye-opening book, *Black is Beautiful*, Dr. Peter Ruckman lists some of the startling, advanced technologies being experimented with:

> This new bunch of barbarians—just as pagan as any B.C. Aztec witch doctor—are engrossed in: elf zapped genes, single phase, speeding DNA transcription, microwave radiation, reciprocal and effective mass tensor points, micro-pyramid structures in "Cu Metal Flakes," ionic crystalline structures, transduction of theta waves, video-drome signals, the earth's Power Grid Vortex, Fluxon, Spinors, Scalars, ULF effects on biosystems, and phase relationships in the wave motions of radio frequencies.[4]

Why are the vast majority of Americans unaware of the electronic cages prepared for them and of the looming loss of our precious heritage of constitutional rights? Jeffrey Baker, in *Cheque Mate: The Game of Princes*, writes:

> America has been dumbed, dulled, and tranquilized into a state of semi-conscious existence. We have become the "Stepford Nation." We look without seeing. We listen without hearing. We experience without feeling. To paraphrase a recent commercial of the past—"I've fallen and I don't want to get up."[5]

Marlin Maddoux, who founded his own radio network and whose conservative, Christian talk show, *Point of View*, is heard on over 300 radio stations daily, believes that the problem lies in the constant barrage of propaganda and misinformation from the media. He began his pro-America, pro-freedom broadcast after he could find virtually no truthful programs on the controlled airwaves.

"Someone needs to speak out! Someone has to give people a way to challenge this propaganda," he decided. "I could sit on the sidelines no longer."[6]

Dr. Peter Ruckman, the well-known pastor from Pensacola, Florida who has authored dozens of excellent books and specializes in defending the King James Bible against attacks by ignorant, so-called "intellectuals," has also identified the controlled media as a bottleneck preventing Americans from receiving accurate and truthful information. He calls it a "News Media Curtain:"

> There was a *"Purple Curtain"* between the Vatican and
> Rome from A.D. 500 to 1996. There was an *"Iron
> Curtain"* over Russia from 1945 to 1992, and there is still
> a *"Bamboo Curtain"* over China...But, in 1996, there is a
> *"News Media Curtain"* that has prevented 200,000,000 to
> 300,000,000 American citizens from finding out what is
> actually going on under their noses...What did *Life, Time,
> Look, Newsweek, USA Today, CBS, NBC, ABC, CNN, US
> News and World Report, Fortune, Omni*, and the *National
> Geographic* magazine (plus 500 "dailies") follow, while
> they professed to be reporting the "news?" It had to be
> lethal, for sixty years of reporting failed to mention one
> time the total and complete destruction of every civil
> right you ever had under the Constitution.[7]

A Monstrous Silicon Octopus

Regrettably, in America today, in spite of our long tradition of constitutional rights, an apathetic citizenry is unaware of the present danger. A frightening behemoth is rising up from the depths of America's hidden SS establishment. Like a vast and monstrous silicon octopus, *Project L.U.C.I.D.* is stretching forth its ominous and threatening, high tech tentacles. Multitudes of unsuspecting, helpless victims will very soon be encircled and crushed by Big Brother's new, Gestapo police state. Who among us can possibly escape the electronic cages now being prepared for all mankind?

Certainly, the powers that be do not intend that anyone escape their fast-developing control systems. CIA Director John Deutsch, a member of the globalist Council on Foreign

Relations, recently proposed the creation of an "Information Warfare Technology Center," to be established in the National Security Agency at Fort Meade, Maryland.[8] In reality, I believe Deutsch was alluding to the creation of the *L.U.C.I.D.* net and associated computer surveillance networks, a project *already* far advanced in its implementation.

Zbigniew Brzezinski, former national security advisor in the Carter White House and a Rockefeller confidant, predicted the coming of what he called the "Technetronic Age." Through computers, wrote Brzezinski in his book, *Between Two Ages*, men's lives and affairs will be minutely supervised:

> Soon it will be possible to assert almost continuous surveillance over the most personal information about the citizen. These files will be subject to instantaneous retrieval by the authorities.[9]

Sounds like a good description of life under the watchful eyes of *L.U.C.I.D.*, doesn't it?

Wizards at Work: Brain Implants

With the advent of the implantable biochip, the *L.U.C.I.D.* cybersystem could quickly become the "inner pathway" to total, human enslavement by Big Brother's mind control police. In *Microwave News*, Craig McCaw, whose McCaw Communications Corporation is a cellular phone giant, is quoted as suggesting that the FCC actually reserve radio wave spectrum for implants the same way the agency does for radio, TV, and cable signals. Since McCaw's corporate empire has now been bought up and merged into the AT&T colossus, Mr. McCaw's comments cannot be passed off as science fiction. *The communications wizards are hard at work developing this capability.*

Andrew Kuper, in his *Fortune* magazine article, "AT&T's $12 Billion Cellular Dream," gave us this dramatic insight:

Craig McCaw is the kind of man who once suggested in all apparent seriousness—as the color drained from the face of a (corporate) PR man in attendance—that the Federal Communications Commission should reserve spectrum for *telepathic communications* to be made possible by *brain implants* he thinks will exist some day.[10]

Kuper's words, "...brain implants he thinks will exist some day," beg comment. In fact, unbeknownst to Kuper, Mr. McCaw was not alluding to some future era, decades hence, in a 21st century America. I believe he meant what he said—that the FCC best start the process *now* for figuring out how to allot frequency spectra for telepathic communications made possible by brain implants *currently being tested* on live, human guinea pigs.

Are brain communication devices and transmitters—biochips—in fact being surgically implanted in human beings? In an earlier chapter, I broached this subject. Adding to that information, I bring your attention to a book by Robert Naeslund now making waves over in Europe. Here is some information sent to me about Naeslund's revealing, new book:

Robert Naeslund's book, *When the State Rapes*, has been drawing a lot of attention around the world. It includes x-ray photographs showing human skulls with a variety of implants. Injectable transmitters are also featured, as well as accounts of elderly people in Naeslund's native Sweden who are getting transmitters injected into their bloodstreams.

Naeslund says the transmitters produce radio waves which induce amnesia and weaken the immune system, leaving the elderly vulnerable to disease.

"The inhumanity of connecting elderly defenseless people unwittingly to computers has been going on for a least ten years," Naeslund writes.

He says there is plenty of proof of the *"advance towards the technocratic society, governed by new social norms that breed inhumanity...As a natural consequence, covert surveillance systems able to control the neurological activity of the brain have been developed in secret and beyond public awareness..."*[11]

Systems Theory: The Occult Technology of Power

The computerization of all aspects of life, especially the financial affairs of men and nations, is what has finally allowed the men of the Illuminati to assemble such an incredible armory of technological weapons. These weapons are now being used to assault the world's few, remaining lines of defense against the conspiracy. Using their phenomenal store of money and capital resources, combined with political influence, the conspirators have been able to knit the world closely in a mosaic of computerized and televised mass media and information exchanges. But as one authority, Robert Lillienfeld, has remarked in his interesting book, *The Rise of Systems Theory*, such a world "will signal the end of diversity and freedom, a homogenization of the globe under man's dominion— or rather, under the dominion of a small, powerful elite."[12]

Now the interesting thing is that systems theory, which Lillienfeld explored in his book published some 15 years ago, is the very essence and is at the core of what I have discovered to be the *occult technology of power*.[13] Lillienfeld cautioned that if a financial and political elite were to take advantage of systems theory in coming years, "bureaucracy and centralization can become the order of the day." The net result would be that the lower ranks, the masses of people, would be "free" but not in a sense that we today define freedom.

Instead, the masses would be free to *obey* the upper ones in authority, free to fall into step with them. In such a system, of course, those who get out-of-step, who refuse to cooperate with the masters who rule over the *computerized bureaucracy*, could not be tolerated. They must become outcasts and rebels, to be hunted down and banished from mature, New Age society.

The conspiratorial group that I have unmasked in my previous books has been able to wield incredible power by buying up and managing sophisticated, computerized systems, especially databanks of financial histories and transactions recorded and stored in memory banks. Through their control of governments, they have also acquired "ownership" of the computerized systems employed by law enforcement, investigative, and spy agencies. The NSA, CIA and FBI databanks, for example, grow larger and larger with trillions of bits of information stored. Privacy in the New Age of information technology has become something to be treasured and enjoyed only by a few who are able to command that the computers of the world not catalog information on them.

Organization X

The conspiracy utilizes social resources as well as technical. A fascinating, little booklet, entitled *Organization X*, published several years ago by *Intelligence Digest* newsletter, outlined the existence of a conspiratorial group such as I have described:

> Our investigations disclose a diversified group (Organization X) which has worldwide links. This group seems to believe that it is so strong that it can afford to use communism without danger that the communists will, in consequence, eliminate it; and that it can afford to use the homosexual movement (which is very powerful) without rotting civilization.
>
> It seems to think that it can use the drug rings as a means to an end without its own personnel becoming involved; that it can exploit sexual aberrations without consequences to itself; and that it can run the main vice

rackets of the big cities without any long-range danger to the structure it wishes to govern.

Over the years, this group has enlisted disgruntled intellectuals, those with a grudge against the old order of society, those in financial need, and those with vices. It has bought up large interests in powerful publishing concerns, in the film industry, in financial houses, and in other institutions. It has devoted immense attention to detail, so that it now controls vital things in every sphere.

It is quietly led under paid civil servants into ventures which require cash. It has made itself popular by taking a prominent place in public sports, in the arts, and in charity. The objective of this group is to achieve absolute power...

This force, which we can call "X," is closely coordinated. It is of one mind; it is in control of immense resources; it is convinced, passionate, efficient, and deadly. It fears only one thing: public opinion. It tries to control this and to stop anyone from arousing it.

The leaders of this force occupy positions of the highest respectability, and the ordinary person would find it hard to believe that the cultured and charming person they meet at the White House...has direct connections with control of the vilest vice rackets of San Francisco, Marseilles, or Glasgow.

Organization X, says the editors of *Intelligence Digest*, will never be investigated by governments. Authorities are afraid to investigate too closely. Moreover, any government which attempted such a task would not survive because every device of propaganda would be employed to destroy it. Still, the *Intelligence Digest* analysts believe that a strong public opinion, if it can be marshalled and aroused, can destroy the design of the conspirators of Organization X. There is no other way, they insist.

Campaigns of Intimidation and Silencing

Certainly, the media of the democratic world will never expose the roots of the conspiracy. Those few, courageous men and women who have had the audacity and the boldness to attempt to expose the conspiracy and its designs have inevitably been the victims of vicious, smear campaigns to intimidate, harass, misinform, and misdirect. If all else fails, murder, assassination, and kidnapping are used to silence those impudent enough to unmask the most sensitive parts of the conspirator's plan.

I am not unaware of the power that the Illuminati fraternity has to damage me or to ruin my good name and harm my family. Were it not for the fact that I trust in an Almighty God to protect and watch over me, I would be filled with fright and constantly be on the alert, perpetually looking over my back shoulder for who's there. But I am neither scared nor intimidated by these men and their minions. My writing and publishing of books and investigative exposés is proof, I believe, that God is watching over me. I realize the limitless resources of the conspirators, but I am thankful for the many friends and colleagues whom, I know, would willingly stand behind me if, due to the revelations in *Project L.U.C.I.D.*, the establishment powers launch a campaign against me.

"October Surprise" Verified

While the media establishment of the West is too frightened and cowed to disturb the safe nest of the Illuminati, those in countries and systems opposed to the conspirators have sounded many warnings. For example, Abol Hassan Bani-Sadr, the first president of the Islamic Republic of Iran, and the moderate politician who headed up the Iranian government during the time the U.S. hostages were being held at the U.S. Embassy in Teheran, wrote an insightful book in 1991 which touched on the power of the global Illuminati to cut secret deals with foreign governments.

Bani-Sadr verified that there was, indeed, an "October Surprise" plot by Reagan campaign lieutenant William Casey—later to become head of the Reagan administration's Central Intelligence Agency—and others to win the release of American hostages. The plot was intended to delay their release until *after* Reagan had won the election and was inaugurated.

Bani-Sadr, who went into exile after incurring the wrath of the Ayatollahs and falling into disfavor in Iranian religious and political circles, in news conferences promoting his book, *My Turn to Speak: Iran, the Revolution and Secret Deals With the United States,* alleges that a special group of unidentified men are able to control the world's foreign policy through their own, independent "centers of power." These men, he said, do not have to work through government organizations or diplomatic channels, but have their own network and agents in capitals and major cities across the globe.

The United States media mounted a disgusting campaign to paint Abol Bani-Sadr as some kind of self-serving nut out to make a buck on his book. But his account squared with what so many who have studied the conspiracy have, themselves, discovered in recent years.

Ringleaders in the Shadows

Another man who shed some light on the world conspiracy is less credible than Bani-Sadr. That man, the late Erich Honecker, was the Communist leader of East Germany. While in exile in the former Soviet bloc, Honecker said that his Communist regime was overthrown in 1989 by "a vast plot whose ringleaders are still in the shadows."

Honecker also warned: "We are now—that is the reality—on the way to the *Fourth Reich,* a reich in which capital (money) is the real ruler sitting at the levers of power."

We're tempted to disbelieve a despicable man like Honecker when he hints of a vast plot, with greedy ringleaders still in the shadows, deliberately moving us into a terrible Fourth Reich. Honecker, after all, is the man whose dreaded *Stasi* security police kept files on millions of citizens and who ordered security guards to shoot to kill East German refugees attempting to flee that Communist country by scaling the Berlin Wall. But his suggestion of a vast plot of ringleaders does strike me as the truth.

It would have been just as easy for Honecker to simply blame his being toppled on the machinations of such politicians as Germany's Chancellor Helmut Kohl, then U.S. President George Bush, or then Soviet leader Mikhail Gorbachev. These three, renowned world leaders have certainly not shown any remorse—nor should they—for Honecker's being forced to step down. The description, then, by Honecker of ringleaders unknown, who lurk about the "shadows" and who constitute a Fourth Reich ruled by money, deserves our attention.

The New Group of World Servers

Bani-Sadr's description of a conspiratorial organization with "centers" around the globe parallels the actual organization of the Illuminati. What's more, it coincides with the description given by two of the more prominent occult groups involved in the world conspiracy—the Lucis Trust and World Goodwill. In the Lucis Trust book, *Serving Humanity*, we find that the head of the conspiratorial octopus—the *New Group of World Servers*, a Lucis Trust code phrase for the Illuminati elite, is decentralized and hidden from view, and thus, difficult to detect and combat:

> The New Group of World Servers is not an organization. It has no headquarters but only units of service throughout the world...It has only servers in every country.[14]

Keep in mind that the Lucis Trust declaration that the New Group of World Servers (NGWS) "is not an organization," is merely a thinly-veiled attempt to deceive the unwitting.

Indeed, in the same manual, *Serving Humanity*, on page 299, we read that the NGWS "will and should become a strong united body in the world." On page 298, we are told that the goal of this leadership group is that of "providing a center of light within the world of men;" and on page 306, the author reveals that their purpose is "to provide in every country, and eventually in every city, a *central bureau*."[15]

The work of this hidden elite, we discover, also includes propaganda. This is carried forward through pamphlets, personal contacts, and correspondence, through lectures and discussions.[16] The media are also used: "As far as the use of the press...go forward as actively and earnestly as possible...for by them (the media) the majority of human beings are reached."[17]

With command of the media and favorable access to government authorities, *Serving Humanity* notes, the elite are able to exercise their power immediately when the need arises:

> They will be able to swing into activity at any moment such a weight of thought and such a momentous public opinion, that they will...be in a position to definitely affect world affairs.[18]

A Central Command Post

Obviously, this requires a gigantic network of organizations and groups coordinated from a *central command post*. But, at all times, it is necessary to maintain the myth that such activities are *not* centrally controlled and directed, that they happen spontaneously as a response to an informed public opinion. The truth will be quite the opposite but, as Alice Bailey's revealing book states, "One of the essential conditions imposed on the personnel of this group is that...they must work behind the scenes as do the Great

Ones."[19] (The "Great Ones" are spirit guides, or, as the Bible calls them, devils!)

Only by concealing its plan, by remaining hidden, and by maintaining the ability to plausibly deny that a hierarchically directed, global organization even exists, can the Illuminati accomplish its task. In *Serving Humanity* we find that goal defined as follows: "Their task is to usher in the New Age...one humanity...One World."[20]

Have No Fear As Planet Races Toward Disaster

Dark storm clouds can be seen on the horizon. Strong winds of violence are gathering. If you are filled with God's Holy Spirit and possess understanding, you can feel it in the air. Clearly, those who stand solidly for Truth and who refuse to bow their knees to Baal are targeted for destruction.

The unseen men who rule the world are determined to bring in their New World Order by the magical year 2000—the advent of a New Millennium. The introduction of *Project L.U.C.I.D.*, with its technological powers of electronic control, is an ominous sign pointing to the coming, great chaos.

This will fulfill Bible prophecy, for our Lord warned us the time would come when the very denizens of hell would lash out and attempt to destroy God's people:

And it was given unto him (the beast) to make war with the saints, and to overcome them: and power was given him over all kindreds, and tongues, and nations. (Revelation 13:7)

Should this induce dread and fear in us? Are we to quake and quiver at the prospect of unholy *Jihad*—war!— being waged against us by the Satanic, New world Order forces of Big Brother Government?

Absolutely not! An inspired Apostle Paul wrote: "God hath not given us the spirit of fear; but of power, and of love, and of a sound mind" (II Timothy 1:7). For the confident Christian, fear of evil is out of the question. The Bible says that we are the *overcomers*, not the defeated (Revelation 21:7). Though we may individually be weak, our God is strong and He prevails. He is our shield.

Let, then, the elitist men and women who defy God and who seek to persecute true patriots and Christians be fearful. They do, in fact, have much of which to be afraid. God shall be their judge and shall reward them in full for their exceedingly evil deeds:

> But the fearful, and unbelieving, and the abominable, and murderers, and whoremongers, and sorcerers, and idolaters, and all liars, shall have their part in the lake which burneth with fire and brimstone: which is the second death. (Revelation 21:8)

Now, a word to the pseudo-Christians—the lukewarm, devilish pretenders to the faith who enjoy mouthing slogans about "love" and "peace" and who constantly coverup the evil works of Big Brother and his associates in a vain attempt to curry political and economic favor. We all are plagued by these cowards and deceivers in our midst. This I say to them: Don't think you can escape the coming fires of chaos. By your compromises and your embracing of the Lie, you have entered into a "covenant with death" and an "agreement with hell." Therefore, "when the overflowing scourge shall pass through, then ye shall be trodden down by it" (Isaiah 28:17-18).

To the small group of overcomers—and I believe that most of you reading this book fall into this category—I say: Take courage. Heed the words of Christ Jesus: "And fear not them which kill the body, but are not able to kill the soul...But the very hairs of your head are all numbered. Fear ye not therefore..." (Matthew 10:28-31). So we see that God is with us even in times of persecution and pain. He bought us with His blood. He loves us. Trust in Him who casts out all fear. *Only Believe.*

Covert Operations of the U.S. National Security Agency

The following document comprises evidence for a lawsuit filed at the United States Courthouse in Washington, D.C., by John St. Clair Akwei against the National Security Agency, Ft George G. Meade, Maryland (Civil Action 92-0449), and constitutes his knowledge of the National Security Agency's structure, national security activities, proprietary technologies and covert operations to monitor individual citizens. This document reveals a frightening array of technologies and programs designed to monitor and control individuals. (NOTE: This lawsuit brief was printed in its entirety in Nexus magazine, April-May 1996, for which we give acknowledgment.)

**John St Clair Akwei vs National Security Agency
Ft George G. Meade, MD, USA (Civil Action 92-0449)**

1. **THE NSA'S MISSION AND DOMESTIC INTELLIGENCE OPERATION**

- **Communications Intelligence (COMINT)**

Blanket coverage of all electronic communications in the US and the world to ensure national security. The NSA at Ft Meade, Maryland has had the most advanced computers in the world since the early 1960s. NSA technology is developed and implemented in secret from private corporations, academia and the general public.

- **Signals Intelligence (SIGINT)**

The Signals Intelligence mission of the NSA has evolved into a program of decoding EMF waves in the environment for wirelessly tapping into computers and tracking persons with the electrical currents in their bodies. Signals Intelligence is based on the fact that everything in the environment with an electric current in it has a magnetic flux around it which gives off EMF waves. The NSA/DoD (Department of Defense) has developed proprietary advanced digital equipment which can remotely analyze all objects, whether manmade or organic, that have electrical activity.

- **Domestic Intelligence (DOMINT)**

The NSA has records on all US citizens. The NSA gathers information on US citizens who might be of interest to any of the over 50,000 NSA agents (HUMINT). These agents are authorized by executive order to spy on anyone. The NSA has a permanent national security anti-terrorist surveillance network in place. This surveillance network is completely disguised and hidden from the public.

Tracking individuals in the US is easily and cost-effectively implemented with the NSA's electronic surveillance network. This network (DOMINT) covers the entire US, involves tens of thousands of NSA personnel, and tracks millions of persons simultaneously. Cost-effective implementation of operations is assured by NSA computer technology designed to minimize operations costs.

NSA personnel serve in quasi-public positions in their communities and run cover business and legitimate businesses that can inform the intelligence community of persons they would want to track. NSA personnel in the community usually have cover identities such as social workers, lawyers and business owners.

- **Individual Citizens Occasionally Targeted for Surveillance by Independently-Operating NSA Personnel**

NSA personnel can control the lives of hundreds of

individuals in the US by using the NSA's domestic intelligence network and cover businesses. The operations independently run by them can sometimes go beyond the bounds of law. Long-term control and sabotage of tens of thousands of unwitting citizens by NSA operatives is likely to happen. NSA DOMINT has the ability to assassinate US citizens covertly or run covert psychological control operations to cause subjects to be diagnosed with ill mental health.

2. NSA'S DOMESTIC ELECTRONIC SURVEILLANCE NETWORK

As of the early 1960s, the most advanced computers in the world were at the NSA, Ft Meade. Research breakthroughs with these computers were kept for the NSA. At the present time the NSA has nanotechnology computers that are 15 years ahead of present computer technology.

The NSA obtains blanket coverage of information in the US by using advanced computers that use artificial intelligence to screen all communications, regardless of medium, for key words that should be brought to the attention of NSA agents/ cryptologists. These computers monitor all communications at the transmitting and receiving ends. This blanket coverage of the US is a result of the NSA's Signals Intelligence (SIGINT) mission.

The NSA's electronic surveillance network is based on a cellular arrangement of devices that can monitor the entire EMF spectrum. This equipment was developed, implemented and kept secret in the same manner as other electronic warfare programs.

- **Signals Intelligence Remote Computer Tampering**

The NSA keeps track of all PCs and other computers sold in the US. This is an integral part of the Domestic Intelligence network.

The NSA's EMF equipment can tune in RF emissions from personal computer circuit boards (while filtering out emissions from monitors and power supplies). The RF emission from PC circuit boards contains digital information in the PC. Coded RF waves from the NSA's equipment can resonate PC circuits and change data in the PCs. Thus the NSA can gain wireless modem-style entry into any computer in the country for surveillance or anti-terrorist electronic warfare.

- **Detecting EMF Fields in Humans for Surveillance**

A subject's bioelectric field can be remotely detected, so subjects can be monitored anywhere they are. With special EMF equipment NSA cryptologists can remotely read evoked potentials (from EEGs). These can be decoded into a person's brain-states and thoughts. The subject is then perfectly monitored from a distance.

NSA personnel can dial up any individual in the country on the Signals Intelligence EMF scanning network and the NSA's computers will then pinpoint and track that person 24 hours a day. The NSA can pick out and track anyone in the US.

3. NSA SIGNALS INTELLIGENCE USE OF EMF BRAIN STIMULATION

NSA Signals Intelligence uses EMF Brain Stimulation for Remote Neural Monitoring (RNM) and Electronic Brain Link (EBL). EMF Brain Stimulation has been in development since the MKULTRA program of the early 1950s, which included neurological research into radiation (non-ionizing EMF) and bioelectric research and development. The resulting secret technology is categorized at the National Security Archives as "Radiation Intelligence," defined as "information from unintentionally emanated electromagnetic waves in the environment, not including radioactivity or nuclear detonation."

Signals Intelligence implemented and kept this technology secret in the same manner as other electronic warfare programs of the US Government. The NSA monitors available information about this technology and withholds scientific research from the public. There are also international intelligence agreements to keep this technology secret.

The NSA has proprietary electronic equipment that analyzes electrical activity in humans from a distance. NSA computer-generated brain mapping can continuously monitor all of the electrical activity in the brain. The NSA records and decodes individual brain maps (of hundreds of thousands of persons) for national security purposes. EMF Brain Stimulation is also secretly used by the military for brain-to-computer link (in military fighter aircraft, for example).

For electronic surveillance purposes, electrical activity in the speech center of the brain can be translated into the subject's verbal thoughts. RNM can send encoded signals to the brain's auditory cortex, thus allowing audio communications direct to the brain (bypassing the ears). NSA operatives can use this covertly to debilitate subjects by simulating auditory hallucinations characteristic of paranoid schizophrenia.

Without any contact with the subject, Remote Neural Monitoring can map out electrical activity from the visual cortex of a subject's brain and show images from the subject's brain on a video monitor. NSA operatives see what the surveillance subject's eyes are seeing. Visual memory can also be seen. RNM can send images direct to the visual cortex, bypassing the eyes and optic nerves. NSA operatives can use this surreptitiously to put images into a surveillance subject's brain while they are in REM sleep for brain-programming purposes.

- **Capabilities of NSA Operatives Using RNM**

There has been a Signals Intelligence network in the US since the 1940s. The NSA, Ft Meade has in place a vast, two-way, wireless RNM system which is used to track subjects and non-invasively monitor audiovisual information in their brains. This is all done with no physical contact with the subject. RNM is the ultimate method of surveillance and domestic intelligence. Speech, 3D sound, and subliminal audio can be sent to the auditory cortex of the subject's brain (bypassing the ears), and images can be sent into the visual cortex. RNM can alter a subject's perceptions, moods, and motor control.

Speech cortex/auditory cortex link has become the ultimate communications system for the intelligence community. RNM allows for a complete audiovisual brain-to-brain link or brain-to-computer link.

4. **NATIONAL SECURITY AGENCY SIGNALS INTELLIGENCE ELECTRONIC BRAIN LINK TECHNOLOGY**

NSA SIGINT can remotely detect, identify and monitor a person's bioelectric fields.

The NSA's Signals Intelligence has the proprietary ability

to monitor, remotely and non-invasively, information in the human brain by digitally decoding the evoked potentials in the 30-50 Hz, 5 milliwatt electromagnetic emissions from the brain.

Neuronal activity in the brain creates a shifting electrical pattern that has a shifting magnetic flux. This magnetic flux puts out a constant 30-50 Hz, 5 milliwatt electromagnetic (EMF) wave. Contained in the electromagnetic emission from the brain are spikes and patterns called "evoked potentials."

Every thought, reaction, motor command, auditory event, and visual image in the brain has a corresponding "evoked potential" or set of "evoked potentials." The EMF emission from the brain can be decoded into the current thoughts, images and sounds in the subject's brain.

NSA SIGINT uses EMF-transmitted Brain Stimulation as a communications system to transmit information (as well as nervous system messages) to intelligence agents and also to transmit to the brains of covert operations subjects (on a non-perceptible level).

EMF Brain Stimulation works by sending a complexly coded and pulsed electromagnetic signal to trigger evoked potentials (events) in the brain, thereby forming sound and visual images in the brain's neural circuits. EMF Brain Stimulation can also change a person's brain-states and affect motor control.

Two-way electronic Brain Link is done by remotely monitoring neural audiovisual information while transmitting sound to the auditory cortex (bypassing the ears) and transmitting faint images to the visual cortex (bypassing the optic nerves and eyes). The images appear as floating 2D screens in the brain.

Two-way electronic Brain Link has become the ultimate communications system for CIA/NSA personnel. Remote neural monitoring (RNM, remotely monitoring bioelectric information in the human brain) has become the ultimate surveillance system. It is used by a limited number of agents in the US Intelligence Community.

5. [NO HEADING IN ORIGINAL DOCUMENT]

RNM requires decoding the resonance frequency of each specific brain area. That frequency is then modulated in order to impose information in that specific brain area.

The frequency to which the various brain areas respond varies from 3 Hz to 50 Hz. Only NSA Signals Intelligence modulates signals in this frequency band. (See Table 1.)

Table 1: An Example of EMF Brain Stimulation		
Brain Area	Bioelectric Resonance Frequency	Information Induced Through Modulation
Motor Control Cortex	10 Hz	Motor impulse coordination
Auditory Cortex	15 Hz	Sound which bypasses the ears
Visual Cortex	25 Hz	Images in the brain bypassing the eyes
Somatosensory	9 Hz	Phantom touch sense
Thought Center	20 Hz	Imposed subconscious thoughts

This modulated information can be put into the brain at varying intensities from subliminal to perceptible.

Each person's brain has a unique set of bioelectric resonance/entrainment frequencies. Sending audio information to a person's brain at the frequency of another person's auditory cortex would result in that audio information not being perceived.

The Plaintiff learned of RNM by being in two-way RNM contact with the Kinnecome group at the NSA, Ft Meade.

They used RNM 3D sound direct to the brain to harass the Plaintiff from 10/90 to 5/91.

As of 5/91 they have had two-way RNM communications with the Plaintiff and have used RNM to attempt to incapacitate the Plaintiff and hinder the Plaintiff from going to the authorities about their activities against the Plaintiff in the last 12 years.

The Kinnecome group has about 100 persons working 24 hours a day at Ft Meade. They have also brain-tapped persons the Plaintiff is in contact with to keep the Plaintiff isolated. This is the first time ever that a private citizen has been harassed with RNM and has been able to bring a lawsuit against NSA personnel misusing this intelligence operations method.

6. NSA TECHNIQUES AND RESOURCES

Remote monitoring/tracking of individuals in any location, inside any building, continuously, anywhere in the country.

A system for inexpensive implementation of these operations allows for thousands of persons in every community to be spied on constantly by the NSA.

- **Remote RNM Devices**

NSA's RNM equipment remotely reads the evoked potentials (EEGs) of the human brain for tracking individuals, and can send messages through the nervous systems to affect their performance.

RNM can electronically identify individuals and track them anywhere in the US. This equipment is on a network and is used for domestic intelligence operations, government security and military base security, and in case of bioelectric warfare.

- **Spotters and Walk-Bys in Metropolitan Areas**

Tens of thousands of persons in each area working as spotters and neighborhood/businessplace spies (sometimes unwittingly) following and checking on subjects who have been identified for covert control by NSA personnel.

Agents working out of offices can be in constant communication with spotters who are keeping track of the NSA's thousands of subjects in public.

NSA agents in remote offices can instantly identify (using RNM) any individual spotted in public who is in contact with surveillance subject.

- **Chemicals and Drugs into Residential Buildings with Hidden, NSA-Installed and Maintained Plastic Plumbing Lines**

The NSA has kits for running lines into residential tap water and air ducts of subjects for the delivery of drugs (such as sleeping gas or brainwashing-aiding drugs). This is an outgrowth of CIA pharmapsychology (psychopharmacology).

- **Brief Overview of Proprietary US Intelligence/Anti-Terrorist Equipment Mentioned**

Fixed network of special EMF equipment that can read EEGs in human brains and identify/track individuals by using digital computers. ESB (Electrical Stimulation to the Brain) via EMF signal from the NSA Signals Intelligence is used to control subjects.

EMF equipment that gathers information from PC circuit

boards by deciphering RF emissions, thereby gaining wireless modem-style entry into any personal computer in the country.

All equipment hidden, all technology secret, all scientific research unreported (as in electronic warfare research).

Not known to the public at all, yet complete and thorough implementation of this method of domestic intelligence has been in place since the early 1980s.

RESOURCES

These publications have only been discovered since December 1991, after Plaintiff had already notified authorities (Dept. of Justice, etc.) of Public Corruption by named NSA employees. When no action was taken against the NSA employees, I researched the Intelligence Community electronic surveillance technology involved and discovered the following publications.

The Body Electric: Electromagnetism and the Foundation of Life, by Robert Becker, M.D. Monitoring neuroelectric information in the brain; EM waves; ESB (pp. 265, 313, 318).

Cross Currents, by Robert Becker. Simulating auditory hallucinations (pp. 70, 78, 105, 210, 216, 220, 242, 299, 303). Remote computer tampering using the RF emissions from the logic board (p. 174).

Currents of Death, by Paul Brodeur. Driving brain electrical activity with external EM; magnetophosphenes; Delgado (pp. 27, 93).

The Zapping of America, by Paul Brodeur, DoD EM ESB research; simulating auditory hallucinations.

Of Mice, Men and Molecules, by John H. Heller, 1963. Bioelectricity; probing the brain with EM waves (p. 110).

The Three-Pound Universe, by Judith Hooper. CIA EEG research; EEGs for surveillance (pp. 29, 132, 137).

In the Palaces of Memory, by George Johnson. EM emissions from the brain; the brain as an open electromagnetic circuit.

The Puzzle Palace, by James Bamford. Signals intelligence; most advanced computers in the early sixties.

The US Intelligence Community. Glossary terms at National Security Archives: Radiation Intelligence (information from unintentionally emanated electromagnetic energy, excluding radioactive sources).

The Search for the "Manchurian Candidate," by John Marks. Electrical or radio stimulation to the brain; CIA R&D in bioelectrics (p. 227).

Secret Agenda, by Jim Hougan. National security cult groups.

Crimes of the Intelligence Community, by Morton Halperin. Surreptitious entries; intelligence agents running operations against government workers.

War in the Age of Intelligent Machines. NSA computer supremacy, complete control of information.

Alternate Computers, by Time-Life Books. Molecule computers.

The Mind, by Richard Restak, M.D. EEG Systems, Inc.; decoding brain EM emanations; tracking thoughts on a computer (p. 258).

MedTech, by Lawrence Galton. Triggering events in the brain, direct to auditory cortex signals.

Cyborg, by D. S. Halacy, Jr, 1965. Brain-to-computer link research contracts given out by the US Government.

Psychiatry and the CIA: Victims of Mind Control, by Harvey M. Weinstein, M.D. Dr. Cameron; psychic driving; ultraconceptual communications.

Journey Into Madness: The True Story of Secret CIA Mind Control and Medical Abuse, by Gordon Thomas. Intelligence R&D; Delgado; psychic driving with radio telemetry (pp. 127, 276, 116, 168-69).

Mind Manipulators, by Alan Scheflin and Edward M. Opton. MKULTRA brain research for information-gathering.

The Brain Changers, by Maya Pines. Listening to brain EM emissions (p. 19).

Modern Bioelectricty. Inducing audio in the brain with EM waves; DoD cover-up; EM wave ESB; remote EEGs.

Magnetic Stimulation in Clinical Neurophysiology, by Sudhansu Chokroverty. Magnetophosphenes; images direct to the visual cortex.

The Mind of Man, by Nigel Calder. US Intelligence brain research.

Neuroelectric Society Conference, 1971. Audio direct to the brain with EM waves; two-way remote EEGs.

Brain Control, by Elliot S. Valenstein. ESB; control of individuals.

Towards Century 21, by C. S. Wallia. Brain stimulation for direct-to-brain communications (p. 21).

Mind Wars, by Ron McRae (associate of Jack Anderson). Research into brain-to-brain electronic communications; remote neural EM detection (pp. 62, 106, 136).

Mind Tools, by Rudy Rucker. Brain tapping; communications with varying biomagnetic fields (p. 82).

US News & World Report, Jan 2, 1984. EM wave brain stimulation; intelligence community high tech (p. 38).

Ear Magazine. Article on extremely low frequency radio emissions in the natural environment; radio emissions from the human body.

City Paper, Washington, DC, Jan 17, 1992. Article on FCC and NSA "complete radio spectrum" listening posts.

Frontiers in Science, by Edward Hutchings, Jr, 1958 (p. 48).

Beyond Biofeedback, by Elmer and Alyce Green, 1977 (p. 118).

The Body Quantum, by Fred Alan Wolf.

Cloning: A Biologist Reports, by Robert Gilmore McKinnell. Ethical review of cloning humans.

Hoover's FBI, by former agent William Turner. Routines of electronic surveillance work (p. 280).

July 20, 2019, by Arthur C. Clarke. LIDA; neurophonics; brain-computer link.

MegaBrain, by Michael Hutchison. Brain stimulation with EM waves; CIA research and information control (pp. 107, 108, 117, 120, 123).

The Cult of Information, by Theodore Rosnak, 1986. NSA Directive #145; personal files in computers; computer-automated telephone tapping.

The Body Shop. 1968 implantation of an electrode array on the visual cortex for video direct to the brain; other 1960's research into electronically triggering phosphenes in the brain, thus bypassing the eyes.

Evoked Potentials, by David Regan. Decoding neuroelectric information in the brain.

APPENDIX 2

World Surveillance Headquarters

The report that follows, originally entitled, "National Surveillance," was written by Australia's Peter Sawyer and published in Inside News (P.O. Box 311, Maleny, Queensland 4552, Australia). It first came to my attention when it was printed in the U.S. by LtCol Archibald E. Roberts' Bulletin, the newsletter of the highly respected Committee to Restore the Constitution (P.O. Box 986, Fort Collins, Colorado 80522). This article caused a flurry of activity and a round of vigorous denials, admissions, coverups, and more denials by Australian political leaders. The article contends that (1) America's National Security Agency (NSA) is world surveillance headquarters, and (2) Australia has its own secret "computer centre" facility, linked with the NSA via satellite, which illegally watches over Australia's citizenry.

On a fateful fall day in America, on November 4th, 1952, a new United States government agency quietly, and without fanfare, was brought into existence through presidential decree. Few people in America took much notice; they were in the middle of their elections. It is doubtful any ordinary person in Australia knew anything about it at all, or if they did, placed any significance in the matter. Which is a pity; the birth of the *National Security Agency (NSA)* on that day so long ago, heralded the beginning of the world's most sophisticated and all encompassing surveillance system, and the beginnings of the greatest threat to individual liberty and freedom not only Australia, but the entire planet, will ever see.

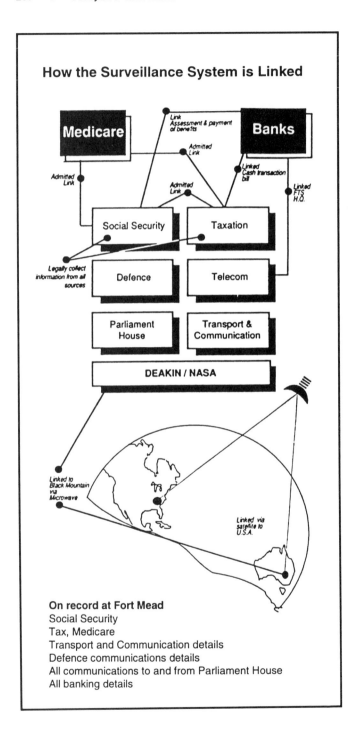

How the Surveillance System is Linked

Medicare

Banks

Link
Assessment & payment
of benefits

Admitted
Link

Admitted
Link

Linked
Cash transaction
bill

Admitted
Link

Linked
FTS
H.Q.

Admitted
Link

Social Security

Taxation

Legally collect
information from all
sources

Defence

Telecom

Parliament
House

Transport &
Communication

DEAKIN / NASA

Linked to
Black Mountain
via
Microwave

Linked via
satellite to
U.S.A.

On record at Fort Mead
Social Security
Tax, Medicare
Transport and Communication details
Defence communications details
All communications to and from Parliament House
All banking details

The NSA grew out of the post war "Signals Intelligence" section of the U.S. Defence Department. It is unique amongst government organizations in America, and indeed, most other countries, in that there are NO specified or defined limits to its powers. The NSA can (and does) do just about whatever it wants, whenever, and wherever it wants. Administration of the organization is by the Office of Communications, better known as "COMSEC." COMSEC is a board of directors consisting of: the Secretary of State; the Secretary of Commerce; the Secretary of the Treasury; the Attorney General; and the Secretaries of each of the Armed Services. The Chairman is the Pentagon's Under Secretary of Defence for Command, Control, Communications, and Intelligence.

Although little known in both the U.S. and elsewhere, the NSA is quite literally the most powerful organization in the world. By comparison, the much better known CIA is but a minor "police arm" of its parent, the NSA. Not limited by any law, and answerable only to the U.S. National Security Council through COMSEC, the NSA now controls an information and surveillance network around the globe that even Orwell, in his novel, "1984," could not have imagined. Most people believe that the current "computer age" grew out of either the space programme or the nuclear weapons race; it did not. ALL significant advances in computer technology over the last thirty years, from the very beginnings of IBM, through to the super computers of today, have been for the NSA. In fact, the world's very first "super computer," the awe-inspiring CRAY, was built to specification for the NSA and installed in their headquarters in 1976. The entire, twentieth century development of computer technology has been the result of the NSA's unquenchable thirst for ever bigger, ever faster machines on which to collect, collate, and cross-reference data on hundreds of millions of honest, law-abiding, and totally unsuspecting individuals. And not only in America, but in many other countries as well. Including, as we shall see, Australia.

World Surveillance H.Q.
Fort Meade, Washington

The NSA's headquarters are at Fort Meade, Washington. Built in 1954 specifically for the NSA, Fort Meade is the second largest building in Washington, overshadowed only by the Pentagon itself. Fort Meade is the hub of an information gathering octopus whose tentacles reach out to the four corners of the earth. The principal means of communicating this information is by the National Aeronautical and Space Administration (NASA) satellite communications system, which most people erroneously think exists primarily for the space programme. It does not. The satellites, indeed NASA and the entire American Space Programme, exist largely to supply the NSA with its telecommunications system. This is why the bulk of its operations are officially declared "secret." Everything else, from astronauts on the moon, to nonstick, teflon frying pans, are mere "spin-offs" of a monstrous plan to be able to monitor every aspect of every person's life in the entire Western world. This effort to build the ultimate "Big Brother" machine, for the ultimate Fascist State, even has an official name, "Project Platform." The European version of Fort Meade is based at Brussels, and the Soviets have a similar computer-surveillance system for the people of the Eastern-Bloc countries. These centres of people control are, in turn, interlinked to each other.

Although the NSA was officially formed in 1952, it grew out of an International Agreement signed in 1947. Officially termed the "UKUSA PACT," this was an agreement between Britain, the U.S.A., Canada, New Zealand, Australia, all the NATO countries, Japan, and Korea. The UKUSA PACT was, quite simply and bluntly, an agreement between these countries to collect and collate information on their respective citizens and to share this information with each other and pass it on to Fort Meade. In order to facilitate this, the agreement laid down a set of common standards for equipment, terminology, intercept procedures, and so-on.

When I first broke the story on the UKUSA PACT in December 1988, there were politicians who publicly stated that such an agreement did not, and never had, existed. Many of these "informed" representatives continue to make this claim even today, despite the fact that the UKUSA PACT has been mentioned in Parliament and its existence confirmed in Hansard. The last time was in 1977 when, on March 9, the then Leader of the Opposition, Mr. Bill Hayden, asked "questions on notice" on the subject. On April 19, the then Prime Minister, Mr. Malcom Fraser, declined to answer the questions, "in the interests of National Security."

The Early Australian Headquarters

That some level of surveillance and monitoring of Australian citizens was carried out right from the start is highly probable, though how, and where, has proved impossible to learn. The first clue of the Australian Headquarters of this unknown infringement of our basic rights appeared in 1975. Then, as today, government undertakings involving expenditure over a certain amount must be presented to a Senate body, the Joint Parliamentary Accounts Committee (JPAC). In 1975, JPAC was asked to examine and approve finance for the construction of a new building in Deakin, a leafy suburb of Canberra a little west of the new Parliament House. This quite massive building was to be constructed behind an existing, much smaller one, which, until then, had been known to the public only as the "Deakin Telephone Exchange."

That it was not, and never had been, simply a "telephone exchange" finally came to light in the 1975 JPAC Approval Report, when it was admitted that the existing building had a comprehensive basement which housed NASA's microwave communications headquarters in Australia. Part of the justification of the "need" for the new, much larger building, was that by 1980, it was expected that NASA would run out of room in their existing home.

Incidentally, despite this document being readily available to anyone who cares to seek it, and despite the fact that approval to commence construction was only given in late 1975, there are STILL politicians, journalists, and television "current affairs" programmes insisting that the edifice was constructed simply "as a telephone exchange," and that it was completed in 1972!

The "old" Deakin "Telephone Exchange" was built in 1966, presumably complete with NASA's basement, so it is safe to assume that this was the Australian headquarters of PROJECT PLATFORM from then, till 1980, when the new, larger building was completed. As another interesting aside, the size of the new Deakin building was largely justified (apart from allowing for NASA's expansion) on the grounds that it would house the telecommunications network for the new Parliament House. Deakin, however, complete with room for this facility, was approved fully six months before Parliament finished "debating" the issue of whether or not the new Parliament House would even be built, which gives you some idea of just how serious the "debate" really was.

The Deakin Centre—Australia's Largest Telephone Exchange

Like its predecessor, the new home for NASA was built under the camouflage of being a "telephone exchange." To this day, there are politicians and "informed" media personalities who insist it was merely built as an exchange, and when it was finished, found to be "superfluous" to Telecom's needs. This, the official explanation goes, is how and why it ended up full of computers.

There are a couple of things wrong with this "official" explanation. First and foremost is the JPAC Report, confirming that the building was meant, amongst other things, to allow for the expansion of NASA's facility. Second, Telecom produced a booklet called "Service and Business Outlook," which details their main expenditure each year, including all outlays for construction over $250,000. Deakin, a multi-multi-million dollar edifice, was built between 1977 and 1980, without Telecom ever showing a SINGLE CENT for construction. I have no idea who ultimately paid for Deakin, but it wasn't Telecom. Not, at least, according to their own financial reports.

Third, and most telling of all, despite the fact that Deakin was not even finished until February 1980, space was being leased out to government departments to house their new "computer headquarters" fully six months before the building was completed. These departments, in turn, had commenced assessing the building's "suitability" up to a year and a half prior to leasing a portion. That is, (if you want to believe the "official" version), Deakin was commenced in late 1977, and by early 1978, before it was even one quarter constructed, had been deemed "superfluous" to Telecom's needs. Again, doubting politicians and media-types can find a full explanation of this assessment process in the 1979 JPAC Report on "MANDATA," another supposedly bungled computer network.

Apart from NASA, it is now admitted that Deakin houses the National Computer Headquarters for, amongst others, the Australian Defence Department, the Australian Taxation Office, the Department of Social Security, the Commonwealth Department of Education, and the Department of Transport and Communications. Both Tax and Social Security are, in turn, directly linked to Medicare. In fact, the Department of Health used Social Security's computer facilities there until their own were completed. A small, but highly significant, part of the building is, in fact, occupied by Telecom. This is the part that contains the networking junctions for the optical-fibre lines leased by the banks for their "Electronic Funds Transfer System" (EFTS). ALL financial transactions by the banks are handled by a subsidiary company, "Funds Transfers Services Pty Ltd." (FTS). The computing headquarters of FTS is just around the corner from the Deakin Centre, in Thesiger Court. We will return to this matter in the next issue. Deakin is also the telecommunication network headquarters for the new Parliament House.

The Political Coverup

When these details first appeared in the *Inside News* in September, 1987, the political reaction was immediate. Statements ranged from "impossible" to "ludicrous." Australia's politicians unanimously agreed that the building was "only" a telephone exchange. Ian Sinclair, then Leader of the National Party, wrote to his constituents assuring them that it was "only" a telephone exchange. Senator Janine Haines, of the Australian Democrats, appeared on morning radio in Sydney with John Tingle and said she had "personally inspected the place, and it was nothing more than a telephone exchange." Mr. Tingle and the good Senator went on to agree that anyone who suggested otherwise, was obviously a "neo-Nazi Fascist," although, to this day, I have been unable to see the connection. Still, according to the Senator, anyone who disagrees with her and the Democrats is some form of "Fascist." It was Senator Haines who referred to Australia's concerned aged pensioners as "a bunch of geriatric Fascists."

Garry Nehl, a National Party politician, flooded Canberra with a five-page story about how people in Sweden had been "conned" into believing that they were all being secretly numbered on the forehead with some kind of laser beam. This, Mr. Nehl said authoritively, was the "kind of nonsense Peter Sawyer was peddling." Little Johnny Howard, then Leader of the Opposition, who never managed to get ANYTHING right, went a step further and actually attributed the Swedish Number story directly to me and repeated the statement that "it was all nonsense." Michael Cobb, a rural Liberal Politician described it as "preposterous." I have no idea if there is any truth in the highly improbable "Swedish" story or not. Through it all, however, Deakin and its billion dollars worth of computer equipment quietly ticked on, amassing data on each and every Australian.

It was not until October 28, 1987, that the first crack appeared in the effort to pass Deakin off simply as a "telephone exchange." On that day, a Liberal Senator from Tasmania, Senator Shirley Walters, released an Australia-wide press-statement to the effect that she had sent one of her staff members to Deakin to inspect the place, only to have that officer run off the site by two ARMED GUARDS, one of whom had demanded the officer's name and personal details and noted his car registration number. On hearing this, the Senator, in her official capacity as a member of the JPAC Committee, had tried to elicit further information about Deakin. She was ultimately referred to the Department of Administrative Services, (DAS) who, strangely enough, was responsible for this "telephone exchange." They, however, couldn't, or wouldn't, disclose any details to her over the phone. Senator Walters had then hauled the DAS authorities before the JPAC Committee, only to be told that all they could say for sure was that Telecom used part of the building. That this was a lie and amounted to contempt of Parliament was later disclosed, but, like everything else connected with Deakin, the fact has been conveniently forgotten. (If the officers questioned meant they were claiming that this was all they actually KNEW about Deakin, they were lying. DAS collects the rent from ALL the departments occupying the building. If they meant that it was all they FELT they could say, they were lying as well, as it has been consistently denied that there is any kind of "security" classification on Deakin and the departments in there.)

Although the Senator's press release was not widely reported, it did, nonetheless, cause something of an uproar amongst concerned Australians, who felt it at least confirmed some of "Peter Sawyer's wild accusations." In another of those strange, little twists that surround the mystery of Deakin, within a week Senator Walters was busy assuring all these concerned individuals that the whole thing had been a "mistake." No officer of her staff had gone to Deakin, nobody had been confronted by armed guards, no one had been asked to leave after having their personal details taken, and there was nothing "suspicious" about the place at all.

Again, from that day to this, the Senator steadfastly refuses to comment on what then prompted her to issue an Australia-wide press release in the first place. Nonetheless, the fact that DAS officers were called before, and lied to, the JPAC Committee, remains forever recorded in that body's reports for anyone to confirm. The matter of claimed absence of armed guards at Deakin raises an interesting question. It is now admitted that Deakin houses the headquarters of the "Defense Signals Directorate," the communications "brain," if you like, of our entire Armed Forces. Our Armed Forces, quite rightly, mount armed guards on EVERY OTHER military installation in the country. Australians, however, are expected to believe that Deakin, which contains the communications "nerve centre" for our entire military operations, isn't nearly as securely guarded as an army depot full of old trucks. Either we are being lied to, or the security of this country is in a VERY bad way.

The First Admissions

That Senator Walters' assurances satisfied nobody was evidenced when the first major breakthrough occurred on November 2, 1987. By that time, enough people were bothering their politicians about Deakin that the matter was raised in Parliament by Mr. Brian Howe, Minister for Social Security, who confirmed that his department's National Computer Headquarters was, in fact, housed at Deakin. Referring to my claims, however, as "bizarre nonsense," Mr. Howe then gave birth to the first "official" story of how this situation came about. According to him, Telecom had designed the building based on "old" technology, but had ended up installing "new" technology, which occupied less space. There had, therefore, been a "bit of spare room" which, just incidentally, was "ideal" for Social Security, and so they had put their computers there.

Mr. Howe didn't get around to mentioning that almost the entire building was "spare room" that housed a whole variety of computers for a number of departments. In fact, everything possible was done to give the impression that Telecom occupied the bulk of the building, and the only other tenant was Social Security, who occupied a relatively small "spare" area. That this story was a complete fabrication from start to finish is now demonstrated by both the 1975 JPAC Report and by subsequent information that is now public knowledge. This, of course, means that Mr. Howe lied to, and mislead, Parliament in his speech, but again, nobody seems keen to mention this fact, not even those malingerers warming the "Opposition" benches. Far from placating anybody, Mr. Howe's speech only further convinced people that "something" was going on, so, on November 17, he had another go, and this time it was admitted that "other" government departments also occupied Deakin; in fact, MOST of the building was filled with computers that had nothing to do with Telecom. This put paid to the "new technology" theory of the "bit of spare space," so a new "logical explanation" was called for. This time it was claimed that Telecom "overestimated" the growth of the Deakin area, and, therefore, had built an exchange far bigger than their needs. Again, this explanation not only defies logic, it is also a demonstrable lie.

The explanation defies logic in that the very small suburb of Deakin, even to this day, is largely declared natural parkland, interspersed with low-density, residential housing. The Deakin building, on the other hand, is one of the largest "telephone exchanges" in the whole country. Do YOU believe this edifice was built as a "local" exchange? Regardless, the explanation is a demonstrable lie. The 1975 JPAC Report approved the building in the first place, not merely as a "suburban telephone exchange," but as the new home for NASA's microwave-link headquarters AND as the communications centre for the new Parliament House. Not to mention Telecom's own records which confirm they never built it anyway. Again, Mr. Howe has been caught lying to and misleading Parliament, and again, nobody, least of all the "Opposition," seems to want to do anything about it.

Mr. Howe's second attempt caused even more consternation than his first. Politicians, particularly the so-called "conservative" ones, were literally bombarded with letters, phone calls, and personal confrontations demanding they fully investigate the Deakin Centre. And so finally, in early December, nearly four months after the first stories appeared in this newsletter, overwhelming public demand forced a group of "Opposition" politicians to actually carry out an inspection of the building.

The Opposition Inspection and Report—an Exercise in Deception

The result of that inspection is now public knowledge. A group of politicians, all of whom only a month previously had been assuring people that Deakin was "merely a telephone exchange," confirmed for themselves that the building was, in fact, the National Computing Headquarters for a whole variety of government departments, including the ones listed earlier in this article. Further, they were shown vast libraries of computer disks, recording most of your "confidential" details. They were even told that all the departments had access to these libraries, which, of course, meant they could (and were) cross-referencing each other's information, something all Australians were absolutely assured could not, and would never, happen, even under the old I.D. Card legislation.

The "Opposition" then prepared a "report" on their visit, again meant to allay people's fears. History will record this "report" as one of the most shameful coverups ever perpetrated by people who had accepted taxpayer's money, supposedly to look after their interests. The report started by stating there were no armed guards on the day of the visit, therefore, there never were any. This is despite the fact that Senator Walters was one of the inspecting politicians. Next, the report CONFIRMED that the building was not a telephone exchange but was principally occupied by computer facilities for a whole host of departments, and CONFIRMED the existence of the disk libraries. The report concluded, however, that there was "nothing necessarily sinister" about all this. The report, supposedly a "well-researched" document, repeated the second "logical explanation" of how this situation came about, in DIRECT conflict with the 1975 JPAC Approval Report, meaning either that document was never consulted, or the information in it was conveniently ignored.

So much for "research." There was "nothing necessarily sinister," according to one of these politicians, because he "couldn't find any wires running across the floor connecting the computers." The implication of all the computers being able to access the SAME disk databases, making such interconnection unnecessary, was completely lost on him.

The report then went on to state as fact that: "The Health Insurance Commission (Medicare) does not physically occupy space in the building, and as far as can be established, has no interconnection with the (sic) Deakin Centre Computer." (Was this simply bad English, or something of a "Freudian slip?" The whole purpose of the exercise, from beginning to end, including the visit and the subsequent report, was to maintain that Deakin was merely, and coincidentally, a random collection of non-interlinked computers. Despite this, the report repeatedly refers to "the" Deakin Centre Computer, as though it was one huge computing facility.)

The report then went into detail about how there was no evidence whatsoever to support the contention that Taxation, Social Security, and Medicare, or any other departments, were in any way linked. These statements, claiming to give Australians the "true story" about Deakin, were made despite the fact that the JPAC, including Shirley Walters, had been told in evidence only a few weeks before that the Health Insurance Commission did, in fact, use the Department of Social Security's computer facilities at Deakin. They were made despite the fact that Mr. Brian Howe, in a letter to ALL politicians in early November, CONFIRMED the cross-link between Social Security and Medicare. They were made despite the fact that the "inspection" was led by Mr. Wilson Tuckey, who had in his possession a letter from Mr. Howe CONFIRMING the cross-linking of Taxation and Social Security records. They were made despite the OBVIOUS connection between Tax and Medicare, given the Medicare levies are collected with income tax receipts. They were made despite the fact that at least some of the politicians present were only too well aware of a vast inter-departmental computer linking system known as "PASS." PASS only eventually became public knowledge in May, 1988, as a result of a court hearing in Perth, W.A.

The "media," ever keen to simply repeat what they are told rather than actually investigate anything, were only too happy to present the politician's press releases as "fact," instead of finding out for themselves. So, despite all the above information, the reports, the letters and so on, being available, they chose, instead, to present Deakin, which to this day is shown on Canberra maps as a "telephone exchange," as simply a big building that just happened by sheer coincidence to end up housing all the government departments relative to the UKUSA PACT, AND our Defence computers, AND NASA.

APPENDIX 3

What is L.U.C.I.D.?

The following article was first printed in Dr. Antony Sutton's newsletter, Phoenix Letter (for subscription information, write to Phoenix Letter, Suite 216C, 1517 14th St. West, Billings, MT 59102). I am grateful to Dr. Sutton for his kind approval for me to republish it in this book.

We live under the rule of law and the basic law that rules the United States is the Constitution confirmed by the Bill of Rights.

The rights to privacy and due process are well established and *almost* universally accepted. We say "almost" because there are disturbing signs that a few elements in Washington, New York, and the academic world place themselves above the Constitution and *have other plans for our future.*

We presume that all contracts let by the Federal Government are checked by Constitutional lawyers for constitutional implications. We presume that academics and universities would not propose a contract that recommended violation of the Constitution. Apparently our presumptions may be in error.

Big Brother planners have now excelled themselves with a totalitarian scheme to hook all of us up to a central computer tracking system, with the assumption that we are all potential criminals and need to be catalogued and tracked.

We have received an article by two academics who should know better but haven't read the Constitution. (To be fair, the senior author is a United Nations officer and may not be a U.S. citizen.) In grand totalitarian style they propose to treat all as criminals and have developed a magnificent plan known as L.U.C.I.D., described as "a concept study for a future Universal Information Identification System."

LUCID proposes that the Universal Biometrics Card, *now under development by the Department of Defense*, be used as "a secure, uniform, interactive and instantaneous tracking system."

Tracking of *whom* you will ask? Not criminals but "noncriminal justice background checks" and "alias criminals." *That means potentially everybody.* (We applaud their ingenious use of the English language. What's an "alias criminal?")

The authors are so bold as to call this a "Universal" system and include "Individual Universal Biometrics Card" on a chart outlining the LUCID System. (The word LUCID is notably close to LUCIS, or Lucifer. We trust this wasn't a Freudian slip on the part of the authors.)

This Big Brother study was written by *Jean-Paul Creusat*, M.D., of the United Nations, New York, and Professor *Anthony S. Halaris* of Iona College, New Rochelle, New York. (Iona is a four year, private, "liberal arts" college founded in 1940, but has no institutional link to the study.)

Lucid is the entire hardware, software, computer machinery framework to handle the UNIVERSAL BIOMETRICS CARD now under development by the Department of Defense. The system transmits encrypted data from remote sensors (i.e., implants and cards).

A card will store more than 5 gigabytes of personalized data with multilingual capability. It can be read into fixed or portable units. In brief, all your personalized data (equal to 100 or so floppy disks) can be received on a small, portable unit in the field from any language, at any time.

The identification techniques used are already developed and, whatever its designers say, *are extraordinarily invasive of personal liberties.*

Within the Universal Biometrics Card will be DNA genotyping and human leukocytes antigen (i.e., through protein material). An iris scan system (i.e., "every iris has a unique stable and highly detailed texture") will be used for personal identification. The eye cannot be surgically altered without impairing vision. An iris code can be analyzed in about 1/10th of a second, say the designers.

What the designers are *not telling you* (as if the above is not bad enough) is that your entire medical history and current medical condition can be read from the iris. This is the little known, but interesting, medical field of iridology. We have been assured personally by doctors we trust who have worked in the iridology field, that the system works. What you are and have been medically is recorded in the iris.

You see the value to Big Brother!

Finally, just to make sure they've got *everything* on you, footprints and fingerprints will also be recorded on your Universal Biometrics Card.

The Smart Card is the preliminary version of the Universal Card and is already in use. Some states are using it for food stamps, others for welfare programs.

The Universal Biometrics Card is a gross invasion of privacy, is unconstitutional, and is presently under development. UNLESS CITIZENS PROTEST TO CONGRESS, IT WILL COME INTO OPERATION.

The Republicans are worse than the Democrats on this one. They have increased the Defense budget funding these control schemes to more than Cold War Days against some *presumed* threat. The presumed threat appears to be *citizens*, not terrorists.

Remember, not a single terrorist incident in the last ten years has been reliably and completely solved. It leaves open the possibility that one or more may be State-sponsored incidents to create the environment for Congressional passage of anti-terrorism legislation.

Something has gone badly wrong in these United States. We suspect it goes back to the educational system under the control of the National Association and the Thomas Dewey (socialist) mentality. These control ideas do not reflect American values, tradition, philosophy—and certainly not the Constitution. These planners are Hegelians. *They believe the State is boss and individuals have to obey the State.* (In Hegel this is twisted to "you find your freedom in *obeying* the State.")

They have to be reminded *sharply* that in the U.S., State powers are delegated by the people, i.e., power comes from the bottom not the top. And any politician who wavers on this needs to be removed from office.

Phoenix Letter Objections to Lucid

1. Law enforcement has a right and a duty to track criminals, that is their function. *Law enforcement has no right to track or*

*collect data on citizens who have not committed a crime unless there
is evidence that they may have broken the law.* This is protected
under the Fourth Amendment. We the people did *not* delegate
the right of privacy to the Federal Government in the Constitution, and it is protected under the Due Process Amendment.

Sure, this makes life difficult for law enforcement, but *that's
what they are paid to do,* catch criminals and stay within the
law. The pleading of "future terrorism" as a reason to infringe
on individual constitutional rights is entirely *unacceptable.* In
the case of LUCID it is *self-serving pleading.* The authors own
LUCID system, and one is President of Advanced Technologies
Group that has financial interest in Big Brother, computer control
systems. *In brief, your loss of personal freedom is their future financial
gain.*

2. The Department of Defense has developed a Universal
Biometrics Card with 5 gigabyte memory. If this is designed
to track *civilians* in some broad, unconstitutional manner, then
Congress needs to remove the funding, *NOW.* DOD has
legitimate functions. *Control of the population* is NOT one of
these functions.

3. These developments have not been investigated by Congress.
They should be and your voice should be heard.

4. A more urgent task for those who would catalog and track
all citizens is to *correct present systems.* The credit reporting
system is jammed with false information. (AND YOU CANNOT
GET IT REMOVED. We have personally tried to have false
information removed for six months without success. One credit
reporting firm—not one of the larger outfits—allowed a
fraudulent ID operator to penetrate the system and plant
information.)

Imagine a LUCID system. Your enemies can plant false
information. The Government can plant false information. The
LUCID system can make individuals anything its operators
want. Unfortunately, the days are gone when we can routinely
trust law enforcement. Waco and Ruby Ridge told us that even
the finest law enforcement agency can be taken over by criminals.
The O. J. Simpson case showed us that police detectives *do* lie.
The Omaha child abuse case tells us that Federal law enforcement
will go along with cover-up and criminal activity.

Do you want a LUCID system in the hands of criminals?

The day that Washington cleans out the cover-ups, investigates the scores of messy episodes, and acquires a *moral approach* to life and work, then, at least, we will listen to proponents for LUCID, if they can overcome the Constitutional question. Which we doubt. The way things are today, we wouldn't trust Washington with a tool like LUCID anymore than we trust O. J. Simpson *or* Detective Mark Furhman to tell the truth.

Footnotes and References

Introduction: *We Knew It Was Coming*

1. George Steiner, *The Permanent Revolution: The French Revolution and Its Legacy* (Chicago, Illinois: University of Chicago Press, 1988). Also see Texe Marrs, *Circle of Intrigue* (Austin, Texas: Living Truth Publishers, 1995); and William F. Jasper, "Fact and Fiction: Sifting Reality From Alarmist Rumors," *The New American* magazine, October 31, 1994, p. 4.

2. George Steiner, *Ibid.*

3. H. D. Corvey and Neil H. McAlister, *Computer Consciousness: Surviving the Automated 80s* (Reading, Massachusetts: Addison-Wesley Publishers, 1980), p. 7.

4. Patrick Henry (1775). This was the same speech in which the patriotic hero of the revolution declared, "Give me liberty or give me death!"

Chapter 1: *Project L.U.C.I.D.—The Beast 666 Universal Human Control System*

1. Antony C. Sutton, "Who are the Criminals?," *Phoenix Letter* (Suite 216-C, 1517 14th Street West, Billings, Montana 59102), Vol. 15, No. 3, March 1996, pp. 1-4.

2. Terry Cook, *Pressing Toward the Mark* newsletter (61535 S. Highway 97, Unit 9, Suite 288, Bend, Oregon 97702), Vol. II, No. 4, April 1996.

3. *Ibid.*

4. Jean-Paul Creusat and Anthony S. Halaris, "L.U.C.I.D. and The Counter-Terrorism Act of 1995," *The Narc Officer,* September/October 1995.

5. Clark Matthews, "Technology and Liberty—Winners and Losers Noted," *Spotlight* newspaper, January 30, 1995, p. 10.

6. *Ibid.*

7. *Ibid.*

8. *Ibid.*

9. Richard J. Boylan, *Perceptions* magazine, May/June 1995, pp. 16-19.

10. *Ibid.*

11. John Monroe, "Federal Agencies Link, Share Databases," *Federal Computer Week,* 1995.

12. *Ibid.*

13. *Ibid.*

14. Clark Matthews, "Snitch Chips, Slave Bracelets, and You," *Mondo 2000* (special magazine issue).

Chapter 2: *No Place Left to Hide*

1. Jean-Paul Creusat and Anthony S. Halaris, "Year 2000 and L.U.C.I.D.® System: A Millstone to Curtail Terrorists and International Organized Crime," *Narc Officer* magazine, (International Narcotic Enforcement Officers Association, Inc., 112 State Street, Albany, New York 12207), July/August 1994; and Creusat and Halaris, "L.U.C.I.D.® and the Counter-Terrorism Act of 1995," September/October 1995, pp. 54-61.

2. Creusat and Halaris, *Ibid.*, L.U.C.I.D.® and the Counter-Terrorism Act of 1995," September/October 1995, pp. 54-61.

3. *Ibid.*

4. *Ibid.*

5. *Ibid.*

6. *Ibid.*

7. *Ibid.*

8. *Ibid.*

9. *Ibid.*

10. *Ibid.*

11. *Ibid.*

12. John Koutsimanis, "Biometrics: Cryptographic Technology," *The Omega Times* (New Zealand), March 6, 1996, p. 6.

13. Creusat and Halaris, *op. cit.*

14. *Ibid.*

15. Ray Nelson, "Computers With a Memory for Faces," *Popular Science,* October 1994, p. 49.

16. Simon Davies, quoted in "The Future, Big Brother, and You," *The Free American,* June 1996, p. 4.

17. "Awesome News" column, *Perceptions* magazine, Spring 1994, p. 48.

18. Robert Hardt, Jr., "Banks Will Soon See Positive Eye-D," *The New York Post,* May 20, 1996.

19. *Ibid.*

20. "DNA Databanks Dot U.S.," Knight-Ridder News Syndicate, published in *Cedar Rapids Gazette,* November 10, 1994.

21. *Ibid.*

22. Simon Davies, *op. cit.*

23. *Ibid.*

24. Antony C. Sutton, "Who Are the Criminals?," *Phoenix Letter,* Vol. 15, No. 3, March 1996.

25. A. K. Chesterton, *The New Unhappy Lords,* third American edition, 1970 (reprinted in 1979).

Chapter 3: *The New MARK Card—"Don't Leave Home Without It!"*

1. Maria Puente, "National Citizen I.D. is Proposed," *USA Today,* July 13, 1994.

2. Rupert Butler, *An Illustrated History of The Gestapo,* 1992.

3. Don McAlvany, *The McAlvany Intelligence Advisor* (P. O. Box 5150, Durango, Colorado 81301), August 1994, p. 8.

4. "Rwandan I.D. Cards Same for Hutus and Tutsis," *San Francisco Chronicle,* June 9, 1995.

5. C. B. Baker, "The New World Order Terror Attack," *Youth Action News* newsletter (P.O. Box 312, Alexandria, Virginia 22313), August 1995.

6. Martin Anderson, "Big Brother's Little Sibling: The Smart Card," *San Jose Mercury News,* (San Jose, California) April 7, 1993.

7. *Ibid.*

8. Don McAlvany, *op. cit.,* p. 9.

9. *Ibid.*

10. Clark Matthews, "Danger in the Mail," *Spotlight* newspaper, June 13, 1994, p. 16.

11. *Ibid.*

12. R. E. McMaster, *The Reaper,* October 7, 1994. Also see Maria Puente, *USA Today,* August 31, 1994.

13. "National I.D. System Proposed," *Perceptions* magazine, January/February 1996, p. 66.

14. *Ibid.*

15. Gary Pelphrey, "Current Crackdown is on Aliens—Who Will be Rounded Up Next?," *Marietta Daily* Journal (Georgia), June 11, 1995.

16. Nick Jesdanun, "Solon: Electronic Fingerprinting Can Prevent Fraud" (Associated Press), *Citizen's Voice,* Wilkes-Barre, Pennsylvania, October 14, 1993, p. 17.

17. Terry Cook, *The Mark of the New World Order* (Second Coming Ministries, Inc,: 61535 S. Hwy 97, Unit 9, Suite 288, Bend, Oregon 97702).

18. *Capital Chronicles* (Box 124, Paconian Springs, Virginia 22129), 1994.

19. Martin Anderson, "Risks That Come With the Health Card," *The Washington Times,* October 4, 1993.

20. Antony Sutton, "Why Clinton Wants Universal Health Care," *Phoenix Letter,* Vol. 13, No. 10, October 1994.

21. Thomas J. DiLorenzo, *The Wall Street Journal,* October 26, 1993, p. A18.

22. *Ibid.*

23. Terry Cook, *op. cit.*

24. "No Privacy," *Spotlight* newspaper, June 3, 1996, p. 2.

25. Jennifer Ferranti, "Marine Worries I.D. is Satanic," *Christianity Today,* 1995. Also on the internet, *America On-Line,* November 21, 1995.

Chapter 4: *Implantable Biochips: A "Do or Die" Situation*

1. Texe Marrs, *Mega Forces: Signs and Wonders of the Coming Chaos* (Austin, Texas: Living Truth Publishers, 1988), pp. 27-28. (The book, *Mega Forces,* is available by order from Living Truth Publishers, phone toll free 1-800-234-9763.)

2. *Ibid.,* p. 85.

3. Texe Marrs, *The Boulder Weekly,* quoted in "Paranoid Reality: Doctor Patents Human 'Biochip', " *Media Bypass* magazine, June 1996, p. 29.

4. Stanley Wellborn, *U.S. News and World Report,* December 31, 1984.

5. G. Harry Stine, *The Silicon Gods* (New York: Dell Publishing Co., Inc., 1984).

6. *Ibid.*

7. Julie Ann Miller, "Chips on the Old Block," *Science News,* June 28, 1986, pp. 408-409.

8. G. Harry Stine, *The Silicon Gods, op. cit.*

9. Pat Cooper, "Naval Research Lab Attempts to Meld Neurons and Chips," *Defense News,* 1995. Also see Jerry E. Bishop, "Nervy Scientists Move Toward Union of Living Brain Cells With Microchips, *The Wall Street Journal,* February 1, 1994.

10. Pat Cooper, *Ibid.*

11. *Ibid.*

12. Pat Cooper and Jerry E. Bishop, *op. cit.*

13. *Ibid.*

14. *Ibid.*

15. Teresa Allen, "Future Shocker: Biochip" *Marin Independent Journal* (California), April 2, 1989.

16. *Ibid.*

17. *Ibid.*

18. *Ibid.*

19. *Ibid.*
20. Glenn Krawczyk, "Mind Control and The New World Order," *Nexus* magazine, February/March 1993, pp. 41-46.
21. "Smart Cards: They Make Our Enslavement So Convenient," *Monetary and Economic Review,* July 1993.
22. "Paranoid Reality: Doctor Patents Human 'Biochip'," *Media Bypass* magazine, June 1996, p. 29.
23. Rod Lewis, "OK Bombing Suspect Claims Biochip Implant," *CE Chronicles* (10878 Westheimer #293, Houston, Texas 77042), April-June 1995, p. 15.
24. *Ibid.*
25. Allen Woodham, *South East Christian Witness* newsletter, February 1996, pp. 5-6.
26. George Orwell, *1984* (New York: New American Library/Signet paperback edition, 1983, originally copyrighted 1949).

Chapter 5: *Mystery Mark of the New Age*

1. Martin Anderson, *San Jose Mercury News, op. cit.*
2. Martin Anderson, *The Washington Times, op. cit.*
3. *Ibid.*
4. Martin Anderson, *Revolution* (New York/San Francisco: Harcourt Brace Jovanovich, 1988).
5. *Ibid.*
6. *Ibid.*
7. *Ibid.*
8. *Ibid.*
9. *The New American,* July 25, 1994. Also see Terry Cook, *Pressing Toward the Mark* newsletter, June 25, 1995, p. 8.
10. "U.S. May Issue I.D. Cards to Citizens," *Orange County Register* newspaper (California), July 13, 1994.
11. *Ibid.*
12. Joann Chiarello Bruso, "Big Brother is Here," *Colorado Christian News,* March 1996, p. 8.
13. *Ibid.*
14. I highly recommend the book, *The New Economic Disorder,* by Larry Bates (Orlando, Florida: Creation House Publishers, 1994). Bates clearly establishes a link between planned economic chaos and the plot for a New World Order. *(The New Economic Disorder* is available from Living Truth Publishers, phone toll free 1-800-234-9673.)
15. The videos, *Fascist Terror Stalking America* and *The Bloodstained Hands of Big Brother Government* are available from Living Truth Publishers, phone toll free 1-800-234-9673.
16. Bob Trefz, "The Inquisition Begins," *Cherith Chronicles,* April-June 1996, pp. 1-2.

Chapter 6: *ISO 9000: The Program to Mark All Mammon on Earth With the Supernatural Number of the Beast*

1. Jackie Cox, "Is Mastering the Confusion of ISO 9000 the Key to the Marketplace?," *American Papermaker,* June 1992.
2. *Ibid.* Also see John T. Rabbit and Peter A. Bereh, *The ISO 9000 Book: A General Competitor's Guide to Compliance and Certification* (Amacom Books); *The Employee Handbook for Organizational Change,* ISBN 0-944002-07-02; Rick Perrett, "Automated

Calibration for ISO 9000," *Quality* magazine, Novermber 1992, pp. 15-20; *Control* magazine, December 1992; "Manufacturing Companies Support Quality Certification," *Houston Post* newspaper, September 5, 1994; Suzan L. Jackson, "ISO 9000 Reduces Cost, Increases Quality at DuPont," *Quality Digest* magazine, February 1992, pp. 57-62; and *Lab Reporter* newspaper, Fisher Scientific, February 1992.

3. Suzan Jackson, quoted by Jackie Cox, *American Papermaker, op, cit.*

4. Jackie Cox, *American Papermaker, op. cit.*

5. *Ibid.*

6. Donald W. Marguardt, *Management Review* magazine, quoted by Jackie Cox, *Ibid.*

7. Jena Story, "Some Firms Say Quality Has No Limit—International Standards Must Be Met," *Nashville Tennessean* newspaper, September 1991.

8. Suzan Jackson, "What You Should Know About ISO 9000," *Training* magazine, May 1992.

9. John Conway, Sr., "International Standards Cover Quality Systems," *Quality* magazine, March 1992.

10. *Ibid.*

11. John Hillkirk, "U.S. Companies Push for Perfection," *USA Today* newspaper, 1996.

12. "Global Bar Code Distribution Standards Completed," *Automatic ID News,* May 1991, p. 10.

Chapter 7: *Blood Money: Corporate Profiteering and the Making of Human Cyberslaves*

1. Alexander Hislop, *The Two Babylons* (Loizeaux Brothers, 1959 edition. Originally published 1836 in England.), pp. 194, 226, 227.

2. Des Griffin, *Midnight Messenger* newspaper, April-May 1996 (published by Emissary Publications, 9205 Clackamas Road, Clackamas, Oregon 97015).

3. *Ibid.*

4. Patrick Regan, "Inside Inferno," *Bell Labs News,* June 3, 1996.

5. Ronald Kane, quoted in *Popular Science,* July 1995, p. 74.

6. *Ibid.*

7. *Ibid.*

8. Dylan Ratigan, Bloomberg Business News, "Lucent Rises 13% on First Day of Trading," article in *Austin American-Statesman* newspaper, April 5, 1996.

9. David Henry and Julie Schmit, "No Fraud, Comparator Chief Insists," *USA Today,* June 3, 1996, p. B1.

Chapter 8: *A Worldwide Project of the Illuminati*

1. Carroll J. Quigley, *Tragedy and Hope: A History of the World in Our Time* (New York: Macmillan & Sons, 1966).

2. Arnold Toynbee, quoted by M. W. Jefferson, *America Under Seige* (Knoxville, Tennessee: Freedom & Liberty Foundation, P.O. Box 12619, Knoxville, Tennessee 37912), p. 90.

3. "French Populist Visits Iraq, Raps American-led Embargo," (report in *Spotlight* newspaper, June 24, 1996, pp. 10-11) of the interview of Jean-Marie Le Pen by host Tom Valentine, *Radio Free America* program.

4. Randall Baer, *Inside the New Age Nightmare* (Lafayette, Louisiana: Huntington House Publishers, 1989).

5. Manly P. Hall, *The Secret Destiny of America* (Los Angeles: Philosophical Research Library, 1972), pp. 23-24.

6. *Nexus* magazine, August-September 1994, p. 6 (Source: Ministry for Justice, The Hague, The Netherlands).

7. *Sunday Mag,* October 1994 (Sydney, Australia).

8. *Japan Times* newspaper, quoted in *Worldwide News Letter,* Dana Point, California 92629, May 1996.

9. *London Free Press* (London, Ontario, Canada), July 15, 1995.

10. *Biometrics Today* magazine, February 1996.

11. *Sydney Morning Herald* (Sydney, Austrialia), June 11, 1994.

12. *Melbourne Age* newspaper (Australia), quoted in *South East Christian Witness* newsletter, May 1996, p. 5.

13. Philip Elmer-Dewitt, "Peddling Big Brother," *Time* magazine, June 24, 1991.

14. *Ibid.*

15. *Ibid.*

16. See Antony C. Sutton, "The Russians Are Coming," *The Phoenix Letter,* Vol. 13, No. 11, November 1994; Don McAlvany, *The McAlvany Intelligence Advisor,* July 1994, p. 23; and article by James Woolsey, *Harvard International Review,* Fall 1994.

17. "Cooperation With Ex-Communist Praised," *The Journal,* New Ulm, Minnesota, July 1, 1994, p. 2A.

18. *Ibid.*

19. *The Daily Telegraph* (London, England), June 8, 1994, p. 1.

20. "Whitehall Looks at Smart ID Card by Year 2000," *The Guardian* (England), January 16, 1995.

21. "I.D. Cards Dropped Over Fears of Revolt," *The Daily Mail,* (London, England), October 9, 1994.

22. Jean-Paul Creusat and Anthony Halaris, *op. cit.*

23. *Ibid.*

24. *Ibid.*

25. *Ibid.*

26. "Europol Delay is Criminal," *The European* newspaper, April 21-27, 1995, p. 8.

27. *Roll Call* newspaper, May 23, 1995.

28. *Ibid.*

29. *Ibid.*

Chapter 9: *Silicon Octopus: Men Trapped Inside Electronic Cages*

1. Dwight L. Kinman, *The World's Last Dictator* (Woodburn, Oregon: Solid Rock Books, Inc., 1995), p. 13. (Note: This book of 322 pages is available by order from Living Truth Publishers, phone toll free 1-800-234-9673).

2. *Ibid.*

3. *Ibid.*

4. Peter Ruckman, *Black is Beautiful* (Pensacola, Florida: Bible Believer's Press, 1995) (Note: This book of 349 pages is available by order from Living Truth Publishers, phone toll free 1-800-234-9673).

5. Jeffrey A. Baker, *Cheque Mate: The Game of Princes* (Springdale, Pennsylvania: Whitaker House, 1993), p. 198.

6. Marlin Maddoux, *Free Speech or Propaganda?* (Nashville, Tennessee: Thomas Nelson Publishers, 1990), p. 18.

7. Peter Ruckman, *op. cit.,* p. 232.

8. John Deutsch, *internet,* June 29, 1996. Also reported by *Associated Press* wire.

9. Zbigniew Brzezinski, *Between Two Ages.*

10. Andrew Kuper, "AT&T's $12 Billion Cellular Dream," *Fortune* magazine, December 12, 1994, p. 102. Also see *Microwave News, November/December 1994.*

11. Robert Naeslund, *When the State Rapes* (address: Robert Naeslund, Slipgaten 12, 117-39, Stockholm, Sweden).

12. Robert Lillienfeld, *The Rise of Systems Theory* (New York: John Wiley & Sons, 1978), pp. 70, 160, 174, and 263.

13. See my (Texe Marrs') books, *Dark Majesty, Millennium,* and *Circle of Intrigue,* for extensive discussions of the Hegelian Dialectic, also called Systems Theory and "The Planned Conflict of Opposites." This diabolical, alchemical system of mind control is employed by the Illuminati and its inferior groups to drive the world toward a Satanic *World Order.*

14. Alice Bailey, *Serving Humanity* (New York: Lucis Publishing Company), p. 293.

15. *Ibid.*

16. *Ibid.,* p. 305.

17. *Ibid.,* p. 302.

18. *Ibid.,* p. 300.

19. *Ibid.,* p. 294.

20. *Ibid.,* p. 297.

For Our Newsletter

Texe Marrs offers a *free* newsletter about Bible prophecy and world events, secret societies, the New Age movement, cults, and the occult challenge to Christianity. If you would like to receive this newsletter, please write to:

Living Truth Ministries
1708 Patterson Road
Austin, Texas   78733

Please e-mail your request to: livingtr@io.com, or visit us at our internet website: http://www.texemarrs.com

About the Author

Well-known author of the #1 national bestseller, *Dark Secrets of The New Age*, **Texe Marrs** has also written 35 other books for such major publishers as Simon & Schuster, John Wiley, Prentice Hall/Arco, Stein & Day, and Dow Jones-Irwin. His books have sold over two million copies.

Texe Marrs was assistant professor of aerospace studies, teaching American defense policy, strategic weapons systems, and related subjects at the University of Texas at Austin for five years. He has also taught international affairs, political science, and psychology for two other universities. A graduate *summa cum laude* from Park College, Kansas City, Missouri, he earned his Master's degree at North Carolina State University.

As a career USAF officer (now retired), he commanded communications-electronics and engineering units. He holds a number of military decorations including the Vietnam Service Medal, and served in Germany, Italy, and throughout Asia.

President of Living Truth Publishers in Austin, Texas, Texe Marrs is a frequent guest on radio and TV talk shows throughout the U.S.A. and Canada. His monthly newsletter, *Flashpoint*, is distributed around the world, and he is also heard globally on his international shortwave radio program, *World of Prophecy*.